NEW DIRECTIONS FOR COMMUNITY COLLEGES

Arthur M. Cohen
EDITOR-IN-CHIEF
Florence B. Brawer
ASSOCIATE EDITOR

WITHDRAWN

Writing Across the Curriculum in Community Colleges

Linda C. Stanley
Queensborough Community College, CUNY

Joanna Ambron
Queensborough Community College, CUNY

EDITORS

Number 73, Spring 1991

JOSSEY-BASS INC., PUBLISHERS
San Francisco

ᵖN
81
.N 757
991

EDUCATIONAL RESOURCES INFORMATION CENTER

Clearinghouse For Junior Colleges

UNIVERSITY OF CALIFORNIA, LOS ANGELES

WRITING ACROSS THE CURRICULUM IN COMMUNITY COLLEGES
Linda C. Stanley, Joanna Ambron (eds.)
New Directions for Community Colleges, no. 73
Volume XIX, number 1
Arthur M. Cohen, Editor-in-Chief
Florence B. Brawer, Associate Editor

© 1991 by Jossey-Bass Inc., Publishers. All rights reserved.

No part of this issue may be reproduced in any form—except for a brief quotation (not to exceed 500 words) in a review or professional work—without permission in writing from the publishers.

Microfilm copies of issues and articles are available in 16mm and 35mm, as well as microfiche in 105mm, through University Microfilms Inc., 300 North Zeeb Road, Ann Arbor, Michigan 48106.

LC 85-644753   ISSN 0194-3081   ISBN 1-55542-785-5

NEW DIRECTIONS FOR COMMUNITY COLLEGES is part of The Jossey-Bass Higher and Adult Education Series and is published quarterly by Jossey-Bass Inc., Publishers (publication number USPS 121-710) in association with the ERIC Clearinghouse for Junior Colleges. Second-class postage paid at San Francisco, California, and at additional mailing offices. Postmaster: Send address changes to Jossey-Bass Inc., Publishers, 350 Sansome Street, San Francisco, California 94104.

THE MATERIAL in this publication is based on work sponsored wholly or in part by the Office of Educational Research and Improvement, U.S. Department of Education, under contract number RI-88-062002. Its contents do not necessarily reflect the views of the Department, or any other agency of the U.S. Government.

EDITORIAL CORRESPONDENCE should be sent to the Editor-in-Chief, Arthur M. Cohen, at the ERIC Clearinghouse for Junior Colleges, University of California, Los Angeles, California 90024.

Cover photograph by Rene Sheret, Los Angeles, California © 1990.

Printed on acid-free paper in the United States of America.

CONTENTS

EDITORS' NOTES

Despite ample and growing information about Writing Across the Curriculum (WAC) theory and practice in higher education, very little has been written about WAC programs in community colleges. This volume addresses that lack, in the hope that program planners and administrators from two-year institutions will discover the elements essential to initiating a WAC program or, alternatively, to determining future direction for one already in existence.

The chapters in this volume take an inductive approach. In Chapter One, Joanna Ambron traces the historical roots of WAC and discusses the suitability of this pedagogical movement to our nation's community colleges. Barbara R. Stout and Joyce N. Magnotto, in Chapter Two, document the occurrence and shape of WAC programs from a national survey of community colleges. In Chapter Three, Lee Odell forges the connection between writing and learning theory and then showcases writing strategies from vocational/technical courses that foster learning and seek to develop a critical acumen.

At this juncture, in Chapter Four, Martin B. Spear, Dennis McGrath, and Evan Seymour pose a dialectic between traditional WAC practices, including English-department sponsorship and such generic writing assignments as journals, and cross-disciplinary sponsorship and discourse-centered writing, that is, writing that is peculiar to science, history, and nursing.

Any new approach to pedagogy requires fundamental changes in the belief systems that concern teaching and learning, as well as in faculty's perceptions of their institutional role. Therefore, faculty development must have a place both in initiating and in sustaining successful WAC programs. In Chapter Five, perspectives from two geographically diverse institutions are presented. Marsha Z. Cummins and Jacqueline Stuchin-Paprin of Bronx Community College delineate process elements in the design of staff development, and Judith R. Lambert of Richland College focuses on administrative support. Julie Bertch and Delryn R. Fleming, in Chapter Six, admit that WAC faculty development workshops vary in style and complexity, but these authors contend that program planners can incorporate certain guidelines into their own idiosyncratic contexts.

Linda C. Stanley, in Chapter Seven, describes the implementation in three subject areas of two writing-to-learn strategies prevalent in the WAC movement: the journal and the microtheme. In Chapter Eight, Hannah Karp Laipson shows how traditional writing assignments in vocational courses can be redesigned and invigorated as a result of WAC staff development. In Chapter Nine, Patricia Durfee, Ann Sova, Libby Bay, Nancy Leech, Robert Fearrien, and Ruth Lucas indicate the successes and failures at their institutions of implementing writing emphasis courses, which are considered by many to be the ultimate goal of WAC programs.

In the present climate of accountability, any new program has an evaluative component as a corollary. In Chapter Ten, Gail Hughes-Wiener and Susan K. Jensen-Cekalla detail the multifaceted nature of WAC program evaluation. In Chapter Eleven, Linda Hirsch, Joanne Nadal, and Linda Shohet illuminate how diverse linguistic environments impose unique configurations on WAC programs. In Chapter Twelve, JoAnn Romeo Anderson, Nora Eisenberg, and Harvey S. Wiener present a cogent rationale and mode of implementation for a broad-based language program that includes speaking, listening, reading, and writing across the curriculum.

Directors of maturing WAC programs who are planning future directions will find the next two chapters especially exciting. In Chapter Thirteen, Christine M. Godwin delineates the components of a program that pairs writing consultants with faculty in technical and allied-health areas to help students with their writing in computer-assisted laboratories. In Chapter Fourteen, Stanley P. Witt relates the evolution of a simple WAC program into an expansive one that hones students' communication skills, forms networks with the business community, and articulates with other educational institutions.

Finally, in Chapter Fifteen, Dana Nicole Williams provides an annotated list of sources and information about WAC programs.

Taken together, these fifteen chapters are a rich source of information about WAC programs in community colleges. Although the configurations, goals, and practices of their programs differ, all the writers whose work is featured here acknowledge the intimate connection between language and learning, as well as the need for improved literacy and communication skills in community college students.

Linda C. Stanley
Joanna Ambron
Editors

Linda C. Stanley is professor of English and director of the English Department writing program at Queensborough Community College, City University of New York. She is also director of the Queensborough Institute of Writing and Critical Thinking, which includes WAC programs at Queensborough and in the Borough of Queens high schools.

Joanna Ambron is associate professor of biology at Queensborough Community College, City University of New York. She has published several articles on writing-to-learn activities in the sciences. She has also served as a consultant in science education and as the science coordinator for the Queensborough Institute for Writing and Critical Thinking.

The WAC philosophy constitutes one approach to coping with underprepared students and providing them with the skills to become lifelong learners and productive citizens.

History of WAC and Its Role in Community Colleges

Joanna Ambron

In her seminal work on the composing process of twelfth graders, Emig (1977) articulates one of the basic tenets of the Writing Across the Curriculum (WAC) movement: namely, that writing can be used as a tool for learning. Through writing, the student discovers meaning and makes connections between new concepts and those already known. It is a unique mode of learning, according to Emig, in the sense that it is multimodal, involving the eye, the hand, and the whole brain. The single act of writing, in which we move the pen across the page, involves us visually, physically, and symbolically. Thus, writing actively engages students in their own learning, and research in education has shown that students who are actively involved demonstrate more effective and meaningful learning (Katz, 1985). Therefore, since writing is central to the learning process, all faculty, not just those in the English department, should endeavor to help students communicate concepts with clarity, meaning, and accuracy.

In this volume, community college WAC programs, infused with the writing-to-learn philosophy, focus on improving writing in courses and preparing students to write on the job, whereas other featured programs encompass all language skills. Regardless of the focus, the common thread throughout the following chapters is that the writing process and the thinking skills of students are intimately connected (see Chapter Three) and that all uses of language are dynamically interrelated.

Despite differences in configuration and goals, the documented success of WAC programs in community colleges (see Chapter Two) attests to the flexibility and suitability of WAC programs in these settings. Indeed, the basic philosophy of WAC—that, through writing, students discover meaning—is especially suited to our nation's open-access community colleges. Despite the weak language skills of some nontraditional students in these institutions, words can be used as *tools for* rather than as *tests of* learning.

Historical Perspective and Rationale for WAC

The familiar directive "Think, then write" guided most of the teaching and use of classroom writing into the early 1960s and reflected an emphasis on the *product-oriented* approach to writing. With this approach, the writer began to write only after formulating a clear idea of what to say and how it should be expressed. According to Hairston (1983), this focus in writing underwent a "paradigm shift" from a product- to a *process-oriented* approach in the late 1950s and early 1960s. This new view of writing as a process holds that writing is an act of discovery for skilled and unskilled writers alike: most writers have only a partial notion of what they want to say when they begin to write, and their ideas develop in the process of writing.

The forces responsible for this paradigm shift in writing theory are both theoretical and concrete and come from inside and outside the academy. A full discussion of all these forces is beyond the scope of this chapter, but some of the more pertinent causes of the demise of the traditional notion can be mentioned here.

As early as 1966, the Anglo-American Seminar on the Teaching of English, held at Dartmouth College, emphasized having children engage directly in the writing process in a nonprescriptive atmosphere. The seminar's eminent participants based their ideas on linguistic research (Vygotsky, 1962) and on research in cognitive psychology (Ryle, 1949) on how learning occurs. These studies, together with others (Piaget, 1967; Bruner, 1971; Flower and Hayes, 1980), indicate that writing is intimately linked with thinking and learning, that success in writing depends on behavior and skills that must be built and reinforced throughout a student's learning career, and that writing skills develop sequentially and hierarchically along with thinking skills. These three conclusions ultimately became the intellectual underpinnings of the WAC philosophy.

In a study of types of writing assignments in London schools, a research team (Britton and others, 1975) found that most writing was done to inform or persuade the reader, a category that the researchers called *transactional.* A subsequent London school project directed by Martin (1976) studied the role of talking and writing in classroom situations. It was found that some situations actually prevented students from undertaking the exploration needed to form new concepts. In this type of situation, the teacher was so intent on receiving the correct answer that a situation was created in which children were not permitted the opportunity to explore or speculate without fear of censure. This study argues for the value of *expressive* language—that is, writing or talking that explains the matter to oneself and is not meant for any other audience. The learning situation must allow students to undertake relatively unsystematic explorations of new ideas without fear of censure. As Martin concludes, "The notion that writing can be an instrument of learning, of reflection, of discovery, rather than merely a means of recording or testing is well understood by writers, but hardly understood at all by teachers, students, or parents" (Martin, 1976, p. 3).

There is no comparable survey of schools in the United States, but preliminary findings in Applebee, Lehr, and Auten's (1981) study of writing in American schools indicate a pattern similar to the British study: transactional writing dominated the composing process, and personal or expressive writing was virtually nonexistent in the sample. The American study examines one additional category, *mechanical writing,* which Britton and others (1975) did not consider in any detail. Mechanical writing is any writing activity that does not involve significant composing on the part of the writer—filling in the blanks, computing, copying, and taking notes. This category constitutes the most frequently assigned writing in American classrooms. Almost all such writing is done so that students can demonstrate to teachers that they know something. Applebee, Lehr, and Auten, as a first step in improving the writing of secondary school students, call for more situations in which writing serves as a tool for learning, rather than as a means of displaying acquired knowledge.

Besides these forces inside the academy, external forces also hastened the demise of the product-oriented approach to writing. These forces are numerous and well documented in the literature on higher education that chronicles the post-World War II era. This literature focuses on the results of the tremendous growth in numbers and diversity among new students after the democratization of higher education with the 1947 President's Commission on Higher Education. The Commission stressed the value of a citizenry with two years of study beyond high school and recommended an increase in the number of community colleges for this purpose. As a result, large numbers of students (adults, minorities, and the educationally disadvantaged) who had formerly been excluded now entered institutions of postsecondary education (from 500,000 to two million between 1950 and 1970).

A second major external force stemmed from the social unrest of the 1960s. Coupled with the democratization of higher education, it produced many changes. Not only was the curriculum fragmented, academic requirements and expectations were also lowered. Writing requirements were among the first to disappear and were replaced with machine-scored objective tests: the age of mechanical writing had arrived on college campuses. A common rationale was that high school graduates lacked basic literacy skills and that teachers in disciplines other than English should not be expected to teach writing. Hence, writing in most college courses was reduced to a passive minimum and consisted of notetaking and short fill-ins. The WAC movement is a reaction to the lack of writing on college campuses.

The emphasis on the product in written discourse failed to address students who had come to higher education after its democratization. This model of writing did not serve nontraditional students in higher education, especially those in open-access institutions—specifically, our nation's community colleges. Hence the paradigm shift in the teaching and use of writing.

Elaine Maimon, a prominent figure in the WAC movement, dates its beginnings from 1974 and 1975, when Carlton College instituted the first faculty development workshops for Writing Across the Curriculum. These took the form of summer seminars in rhetoric for faculty in various disciplines. The seminars ultimately led to curricular revisions that resulted in collegewide responsibility for writing at Carlton. The Carlton program inspired other institutions, both two- and four-year schools, to offer cross-disciplinary workshops in rhetoric. The goal then was to develop WAC programs that would be based on a consistent pedagogical theory. In an interview with Smith (1983-84, p. 12), Maimon states, "On the surface the programs look quite different, but they all have in common the systematic examination of the operative words—writing across the curriculum. The effort led them to redefine writing, curriculum, and the concept of moving across the curriculum."

Writing Across the Curriculum in Community Colleges

As a result of the democratization of higher education and of open-admissions policies, community colleges underwent the most significant changes, both in sheer numbers and in diversity of new students and programs. One consequence was a period of phenomenal growth in community colleges between 1950 and 1970 to accommodate these new students. Moreover, the original mission of the two-year colleges at the turn of the century—to provide an extension of high school education and act as filters to the four-year institutions—was transformed into a comprehensive mission with respect to transfer, vocational, and remedial programs and community education. Finally, the composition of the student body at community colleges was more diverse, at least among nontraditional students, than in any other sector of higher education.

By way of background, some data will serve. First, few community colleges require a minimum grade-point average. Second, fewer than 20 percent require entrance tests. Third, some 30 percent do not even require the high school diploma. Moreover, as the college-age cohort declines, the community colleges are dealt a double blow: the more academically able students are siphoned into four-year institutions, which have now relaxed their entrance requirements and increased their financial aid. Today more than ever, the students coming to community colleges have lower scholastic ability and have taken fewer academic courses (Cohen and Brawer, 1982).

It is estimated that 47 percent of community college enrollees are now over twenty-five years old (Commission on the Future of Community Colleges, 1988). There are more females, minorities, part-time students, and disabled students, many of them drawn from the lower socioeconomic strata. For the welfare of our nation, these diverse students must be provided with the skills necessary to become productive citizens.

How to educate students who are ill prepared to face the rigors of the traditional academic regime constitutes the most formidable challenge of today's community college. The issue becomes more complex in public urban institutions, such as the City University of New York, given budget deficits, student protests of rising tuition, declining enrollments, demoralized faculty, and calls for accountability from state legislators. In view of these external and internal perturbations, can public community colleges continue to maintain their policy of open access and ensure programmatic excellence?

Embedded in our nation's democratic ideals is the belief that access and excellence are not incompatible but interdependent. Therefore, a community college must provide opportunity; and for that opportunity to be genuine, there must be programmatic excellence. To maintain programmatic excellence, teaching practices must be adopted that will facilitate nontraditional students' persistence and achievement (Roueche and others, 1987). WAC programs can be a valuable survival strategy for community colleges.

As elaborated in this volume, WAC programs and philosophy provide one appropriate response to underprepared students and to faculty members who are bewildered about how to cope with them. Two aspects of WAC programs are specifically germane to this discussion: they provide innovative modes of instruction, which are essential in responding to this diverse population with diverse learning styles, and they require faculty development specialists or currently trained staff members who can cope with these new students. WAC provides strategies that actively engage learners by providing forums where inquiry and problem-solving skills can become lifelong, productive resources.

WAC has had some unexpected benefits in that it has reawakened the sense of community that was lost in the self-centered ethos of the 1960s and 1970s. Faculty from diverse disciplines come together and share their concerns about teaching and learning, as well as their effectiveness in meeting the challenges of open-access institutions. WAC serves two of the most urgent needs of today's students as they prepare for their lives in the twenty-first century: effective communication skills and the ability to think critically. Both are essential to lifelong learners in a rapidly changing society.

References

Applebee, A., Lehr, F., and Auten, A. "Learning to Write in the Secondary School: How and Where." *English Journal*, 1981, 70 (5), 78-82.

Britton, J., Burgess, T., Martin, N., McLeod, A., and Rosen, H. *The Development of Writing Abilities.* London: Macmillan, 1975.

Bruner, J. *The Relevance of Education.* New York: Norton, 1971.

Cohen, A., and Brawer, F. *The American Community College.* San Francisco: Jossey-Bass, 1982.

Commission on the Future of Community Colleges. *Building Communities: A Vision for the New Century.* Washington, D.C.: American Association of Community and Junior Colleges, 1988.

Emig, J. "Writing as a Mode of Learning." *College Composition and Communication,* 1977, 28 (2), 122-128.

Flower, L., and Hayes, J. "The Cognition of Discovery: Defining a Rhetorical Problem." *College Composition and Communication,* 1980, 31 (1), 21-32.

Hairston, L. *Getting to the Core of Education in the Omaha Public School System.* Kent, Ohio: National Association for Core Curriculum, Kent State University, 1983. 11 pp. (ED 284 913)

Katz, J. "Teaching Based on Knowledge of Students." In J. Katz (ed.), *Teaching as Though Students Mattered.* New Directions for Teaching and Learning, no. 21. San Francisco: Jossey-Bass, 1985.

Martin, N. *Writing and Learning Across the Curriculum.* London: Ward Lock, 1976.

Piaget, J. *Six Psychological Studies.* New York: Random House, 1967.

Roueche, J. E., Baker, G., III, and Roueche, S. "Open Door or Revolving Door? Open Access and the Community College." *Community, Junior and Technical College Journal,* 1987, 57 (5), 22-26.

Ryle, G. *The Concept of the Mind.* New York: Barnes and Noble, 1949.

Smith, B. "Interview with Elaine Maimon." *Current Issues in Higher Education: Writing Across the Curriculum,* 1983-84, 3, 11-15.

Vygotsky, L. *Thought and Language.* Cambridge, Mass.: MIT Press, 1962.

Joanna Ambron is associate professor of biology at Queensborough Community College, City University of New York. She has published several articles on writing-to-learn activities in the sciences. She has also served as a consultant in science education and as the science coordinator for the Queensborough Institute for Writing and Critical Thinking.

A national survey shows that community colleges have developed WAC programs whose characteristics are specially suited to the two-year colleges.

Building on Realities: WAC Programs at Community Colleges

Barbara R. Stout, Joyce N. Magnotto

In 1987, we surveyed 1,270 institutions on the mailing list of the American Association of Community and Junior Colleges to collect data on Writing Across the Curriculum programs at community colleges (Stout and Magnotto, 1988). Of the more than 400 schools that responded, approximately one-third had active WAC programs, one-third were planning to implement WAC within a year or two, and one-third reported no systematic WAC activities. In this chapter, we present information from 121 colleges with active programs to show the current state of Writing Across the Curriculum at two-year institutions.

Responses to the survey from these 121 colleges reveal that the colleges have implemented a variety of WAC programs, some resembling four-year models but many thoughtfully designed to account for the student diversity, the heavy teaching loads, and the technical and transfer curricula typical at two-year institutions. Such programs are described in this volume and provide useful models for continuing WAC development.

The Survey

The first section of the survey asked for basic information about WAC: the year the program began, program administration, funding arrangements, program activities, and curricular changes. Another section asked about the perceived benefits of WAC. A third section asked for impediments to implementing the program, such as nontraditional students, faculty workloads, and diversity of curricula.

Basic Program Features

There is no single model for WAC at community colleges, yet responses to our survey indicate basic similarities. For example, most community college WAC programs began in the 1980s. Most are directed by faculty members. Most schedule workshops to help faculty use writing more effectively in their teaching. Most lead to curricular change.

Longevity. Formal WAC programs are recent developments at community colleges. Only 7 percent of survey respondents (nine colleges) reported starting before 1979; 43 percent began between 1980 and 1984, 50 percent between 1985 and 1987.

Program Administration. Programs are usually directed by faculty: 47 percent are directed by a full-time faculty member, 19 percent by two or more faculty, and 6 percent by part-time faculty. Twelve percent reported management by a dean or other administrator. The remaining respondents indicated no directors for their programs. Multidisciplinary WAC committees were reported by 66 percent of the respondents.

Funding. Program funding varies in amounts and sources. Annual budgets of $1,000 to $4,000 are common, although 23 percent reported no funding, and 14 percent reported budgets of more than $4,000. Compensation for directors includes release time, varying from less than a course to the full-time reassignment reported by five colleges (4 percent). Twelve percent reported extra pay for a WAC director, ranging from $100 to over $300. Thirty percent of the WAC directors receive no compensation. In contrast, over half the colleges, or 52 percent, have provided stipends to faculty for participation in WAC activities. Institutional operating budgets are the usual source of funding, but some colleges use Title III, Vocational Education, or National Endowment for the Humanities funds. Grants from the Bush, Ford, and Sid W. Richardson Foundations have made possible three of the projects discussed in later chapters of this volume.

WAC Workshops. Faculty development workshops are the mainstay of community college WAC programs. Half-day sessions were reported by 74 percent of the respondents, full-day workshops by 35 percent, and workshops or institutes lasting several days by 31 percent. Three colleges reported semester-long courses or institutes for faculty. Over 60 percent of the colleges have employed outside consultants; 84 percent have developed in-house presentations.

Workshop topics address the learning/literacy focus of the WAC movement, as well as faculty's concerns about writing. "Writing to learn" and "writing and thinking" have received attention at over 70 percent of responding colleges. Fifty percent have provided sessions on "assignment design" and "responding to student writing." Twenty-three percent have dealt with "writing in careers," 16 percent with "correctness."

Additional Activities. Thirty-one percent of the programs have published assignment suggestions or models for faculty; 13 percent have published resource books. Twenty percent produce WAC newsletters. Twenty-two percent encourage faculty writing; 11 percent sponsor faculty writing groups.

Student Support. Colleges with WAC programs often provide support for students. Writing centers and tutoring were identified as WAC-related services at 67 percent of the colleges. Twenty-five percent have sponsored writing workshops for students or have provided other help with writing assignments.

Curricular Changes. Writing Across the Curriculum is frequently related to curriculum development at community colleges. Over one-third of reporting colleges have established connections between WAC and general education or core curricula. About one-third have writing-emphasis courses. Twenty-five percent report revised English composition courses, 20 percent offer team-taught composition/subject courses, and 16 percent report revised remedial programs. Only 16 percent say that WAC has not been part of curriculum development at their colleges.

Benefits of WAC

The investment in WAC has benefited community colleges in three important ways: "more writing outside of English courses" (78 percent), "increased faculty interaction among disciplines" (60 percent), and "increased faculty interaction within disciplines" (60 percent). Half of the respondents believe that WAC has led to improved teaching and learning, and half noted more essay exams as a result of WAC. One-third of the respondents reported improved composition teaching. Almost another third indicated that WAC has increased faculty research, publication, presentations, and interaction with other community colleges. About 10 percent reported increased interaction with four-year colleges and secondary schools, but only four colleges (3 percent) noted increased interaction with employers.

Community College Realities

Because of concerns voiced by colleagues, we included a series of questions about possible impediments to WAC at community colleges—impediments arising from curricular, faculty, and student circumstances typical of two-year, open-admission institutions. Survey respondents were in agreement about problems: 73 percent indicated "heavy teaching loads," 65 percent said that faculty are uncertain about grading or responding to students' writing, and 60 percent indicated "faculty reluctance to change methods or assignments." Fifty-three percent marked "curricula in which writing is not usually assigned," and 50 percent marked "large classes" and "insufficient funding" as possible impediments. Forty percent identified lack of time for professional development activities, as well as large numbers of part-time faculty. Thirty-five percent reported faculty misperceptions about the writing-to-learn concept and about the importance of writing. The same percentage worried about lack of faculty interest. Sixteen percent reported faculty opposition.

Respondents showed sensitivity to the circumstances of community college students, identifying possible student problems related to WAC. Sixty-eight percent cited "heavy job and family demands," and 64 percent cited "wide range of ability." Half of the respondents said that students do not see writing as important, and half also believed that many students suffer some writing anxiety. One-third noted the lack of upper-division students as tutors and role models, and one-quarter expressed concern about addressing the writing needs across the curriculum of non-native speakers of English.

At first glance, the list of impediments seems discouraging. All 121 of the survey respondents with active WAC programs noted one or more of these problems on their campuses. As we reviewed responses, however, we concluded that while we had termed these impediments problems, respondents saw them as simply community college realities. While their effects on program success are unquestionable, most respondents believe that a thoughtfully designed program that accommodates these realities can establish a strong base for future program development.

The Future

In the future, WAC programs must continue to connect writing, thinking, and learning. WAC must reach not only across college disciplines but also across school boundaries to secondary and transfer institutions and across employment boundaries to the businesses that hire graduates. In addition, research and analysis must continue. As other chapters of this volume make clear, WAC programs raise complex questions. Our survey results reassure us that we have made a good start by building WAC programs that account for community college realities and foster community college ideals.

Reference

Stout, B., and Magnotto, J. "Writing Across the Curriculum at Community Colleges." In S. McLeod (ed.), *Strengthening Programs for Writing Across the Curriculum*. New Directions for Teaching and Learning, no. 36. San Francisco: Jossey-Bass, 1988.

Barbara R. Stout is professor of English and coordinator of Writing Across the Curriculum at Montgomery College, Rockville, Takoma Park, and Germantown, Maryland.

Joyce N. Magnotto is associate professor of English studies and coordinator of Writing Across the Curriculum at Prince George's Community College, Largo, Maryland. She serves on the board of consultants of the National Network of WAC Programs.

Instructors in vocational/technical courses should consider using writing (as opposed to teaching writing) as a means of helping students think about and come to their own understanding of the subject matter of particular courses.

On Using Writing

Lee Odell

Everything in this chapter depends on the distinction between teaching writing and using writing to teach vocational/technical subjects. The primary goal of a course is to teach the subject matter. Unless the course is specifically labeled a *writing* course, writing must be a means to an end, not an end in itself. Why use writing? Because writing involves processes of thinking about and making one's own sense of a particular body of subject matter. Given this view of writing, I want to describe some ways in which community college faculty are beginning to use writing to teach the subject matter of vocational and technical courses. Underlying these descriptions are some understandings of the kinds of thinking processes that writing can help promote, thinking processes that are crucial to students' understanding the subject matter of particular courses.

A Definition of Thinking

At the risk of oversimplifying, I will say that current work in thinking can be subsumed under six categories, each representing a basic type of intellectual activity that can help writers and learners examine any sort of subject matter in the hope of arriving at some new insight. As I do so, it will be obvious that I have drawn heavily on a number of sources, most notably from the work of cognitive psychologist Robert J. Sternberg (1986), and from such scholars as Elbow (1975) and Young, Becker, and Pike (1970).

The theoretical position described in this chapter was developed over the course of a three-year project funded by the Sid W. Richardson Foundation.

The first of these activities is *selecting*. It is impossible to attend to everything that goes on around us. Instead, we have to focus our attention on some things and either reduce others to marginal awareness or ignore them altogether. Further, if we are to look really closely at an object or event, we will have to be able to shift focus, moving back and forth between relatively small details and larger outlines.

As a part of focusing our attention, we usually have to *encode* what we are seeing, hearing, or otherwise experiencing. Sometimes this process of encoding is conscious; in conversation, for example, we frequently find ourselves or others remarking "Okay, so what you're saying is. . . ." This paraphrasing is a way of making sure that we have understood someone else's comments. On other occasions, this encoding process is unconscious and affects our ability to comprehend what we are dealing with.

In addition to selecting and encoding, we must also *draw on prior knowledge, values, and experiences*. We do not approach any experience as a blank slate. Even if the subject matter is totally unfamiliar to us, we come to it with knowledge, values, beliefs, and analytical procedures that we have developed over time. To remember and understand any new experience, we have to know the ways in which it does and does not fit in with what we already know.

As we focus on a given topic or phenomenon, we *relate* it to other topics or phenomena; or, confronted with a lot of information, we may need to look for categories and subcategories within the information at hand. Having zeroed in on a fact, an action, a feeling, or a concept, we may need to classify it, label it, see how it is similar to other phenomena or ideas. This effort is often closely linked with attempts to observe how the phenomenon differs from other, comparable things or how it conflicts with what someone hopes, thinks, or expects. We may need to relate a phenomenon to the setting in which it occurs, or to larger sequences: What led up to or caused it? What are its consequences? What if the phenomenon were modified in some way?

In addition to noticing relationships, we also have to *consider alternatives*. This activity is readily apparent in the use of brainstorming: we try to think of as many possibilities—and as many different kinds of possibilities—as we can. Thinking of possibilities necessarily entails a second sort of activity: assessing a particular alternative. We try to think of facts or ideas that will either refute or support a claim, that will justify or repudiate a way of expressing or organizing our ideas. Considering alternatives entails considering perspectives that differ from our own. We inevitably approach any subject from our own perspective, but we can at least enlarge that perspective. We can try to empathize with our readers, anticipating points where readers may disagree or become confused. We can try to consider an event from the perspective of various people who participate in it. When we are inclined to be skeptical, we can momentarily suspend our disbelief, trying to understand the basis of a viewpoint that differs from our own.

Finally, we have to pay attention to what we are doing. The currently popular label for this activity, *metacognition*, simply refers to processes that are familiar enough to all of us, especially when we encounter some difficulty in thinking through a topic. On such occasions, we find ourselves forced to reflect not just on the topic but on the way we are approaching it. Am I making some unwarranted assumptions? Is there another way I could proceed? Exactly what is giving me trouble? Where am I getting confused? Is there any of this that makes sense to me?

In listing these six types of thinking processes, I do not mean to suggest that thinking is a neat, linear activity in which one first selects, then encodes, then draws on prior knowledge, and so on. Nor do I want to suggest that all thought is conscious and rational. Clearly, the processes I have mentioned interact in complex and unpredictable ways. Further, thinking relies heavily on nonrational, intuitive processes that seem unknowable. But I do mean to suggest that some thinking processes *are* conscious. Through our writing assignments, we can help students use some of these processes as they try to make sense of what they hear, see, and read in our courses.

Suggestions for Teaching and Curriculum Development

Working Collaboratively. The attempt to develop and test assignments and teaching strategies will require the collaboration of writing teachers and instructors in other subjects. The task is simply too complex for one group alone; each group has specialized knowledge that the other must have access to. For example, in working with colleagues in another discipline, I can draw on some general principles that describe what students need to do when they think and write. For instance, I know that there are times when a writer needs to think hypothetically, speculating freely about the consequences of a given phenomenon. Moreover, I can show faculty in another discipline how to design and use a writing assignment that will elicit this sort of thinking. But there are things I do not know, questions I cannot answer: On what occasions in a given course is it a good idea to speculate about consequences? What are the topics that invite this sort of work? What constitutes a plausible speculation? Are there types of speculation that are simply inappropriate to a particular subject area? How might this work fit in with the long-range goals of a particular course? These are questions that must be answered if the writing assignment is to succeed, and the only people who can answer them are the faculty of a particular discipline. Neither of us will function well without the other.

Devising Writing Assignments. Listed here are several assignments that have developed out of discussions with vocational/technical faculty at two community colleges in Dallas, Brookhaven College and North Lake College. Although the wording of these assignments may be appropriate for only one specific teaching situation, the assignments reflect an effort to develop types of thinking strategies that may be repeated in other writing assignments and that have some place in the larger scheme of things. All these assignments involve *reflective writing*. They are short, informal assignments that are completed and used while a class is in session. The goal of these assignments is to get ideas down on paper as quickly as possible, not worrying about such matters as paragraphing, sentence structure, or punctuation. As the current academic year unfolds, we also plan to work with ways to use more formal, out-of-class writing to teach the content of vocational/technical courses. In all cases, we will try to make certain that each assignment is clearly related to the long-term goals of the course in which it is assigned. For example, in a carpentry class, the instructor wants students to *see alternatives*, that is, recognize that there may be a lot of potential solutions to a given problem, and to *assess* those alternatives by thinking of consequences, that is, understand that the difference between a good solution and a bad one may be that the bad solution will have a number of undesirable consequences.

Thus, early in the semester, a reflective writing assignment could ask students to brainstorm as many solutions as possible to a given problem. After students write for a few minutes, the whole class may contribute to a list of possible solutions. Then the instructor and the students can talk about which solutions would have the best consequences. After students have done this sort of work once or twice, a subsequent reflective writing assignment might read as follows: "Here is a situation you may encounter on the job, and here are three possible solutions. Consider the consequences of each potential solution, and explain how these consequences lead you to choose one solution over the other."

In a course on office practices, the instructor has spent part of one class talking about computer hardware and software and has assigned readings that describe hardware and software. At the beginning of a subsequent class, the instructor asks students to talk in pairs about the differences between hardware and software. The instructor assumes that the distinction between these two terms is absolutely crucial; if students are confused about these terms, they will have trouble all semester long. Therefore, the instructor may ask students to do some reflective writing in which they accomplish the following tasks:

Select and Encode: Students select relevant information from three different sources and express that information in their own words.
Contrast: In selecting information, they have to identify things that point out differences between hardware and software.

The reflective writing assignment would be as follows: "Thinking back over what you've read and heard for the past few days, explain in your own words the difference between *hardware* and *software.*"

In an engineering class on fluid dynamics, the instructor wants to make certain that students understand the concrete applications of the general laws that are basic to understanding how fluids move through an enclosed space. After lecturing on Bernoulli's law, the instructor gives students this reflective writing assignment: "Assume that a fluid is moving through a pipe with a twelve-inch diameter. What happens to that fluid if the pipe suddenly is constricted to a six-inch diameter? Express your answer in your own words." In this assignment, students have to *select* key ideas from the instructor's lecture on Bernoulli's law, *encode* them in their own language, and *relate* the phenomena that occur in the pipe to the general principles of Bernoulli's law.

Like the other reflective writing assignments described here, this one is a task that can be repeated several times. It probably should be repeated, since it is tied directly to one of this instructor's basic goals, getting students to see the specific applications of the general laws dealt with in the course.

Integrating Writing into the Class Period. Once students have written reflectively, we must do something with their writing. We must use it in some way that advances the work of the class period. The way instructors and students use a particular reflective writing assignment may depend in large part on the nature of the assignment and on our purposes in giving it. If we simply want the writing to reinforce some basic point already expressed or implied in class, we may give students two or three minutes to write, and then we call on several students in turn, asking each to tell briefly the gist of what he or she wrote. Our own response may also be brief, but in all cases it will be kindly and encouraging. In other cases, the writing assignment may be more open-ended, our purposes more complex, and the topic deserving of more attention. We may want to make sure that every student in the class participates in developing a classroom atmosphere in which students feel free to talk to one another about their writing and in which they develop trust in their ability to collaborate in rethinking and revising what they have written. These two instances do not begin to exhaust the variety of ways we and our students can talk about what they have written, but I hope the point is clear: once students have written, we need to do something with that writing, something that will have some immediate benefit both for us and for our students.

Learning from Students. One of the most important things we can do with students' writing is to learn from it. At the very least, an occasional review of students' reflective writing can help us determine whether the messages students are constructing in their own minds bear any resemblance to the messages we hope to communicate. For example, a teacher of an intermediate algebra course asked students to find the absolute value of x in the equation $4x - 6 = 2$ and write a step-by-step explanation of how they would solve the problem. In general, students worked the problem correctly, but in describing what one would need to do at a given step, a number of students incorrectly labeled the operation they were performing. This led the instructor to wonder whether students had simply been imitating a procedure they had just been shown, rather than understanding what each operation was and why it was important in a particular situation. This concern suggested that she needed to ask students to solve and describe additional problems, so that she could get them to recognize the correct use of certain key mathematical terms.

Sometimes close analysis of a piece of writing can clarify our goals for the writing and improve our ability to help students on subsequent assignments. For example, a nursing instructor frequently asked students to write brief summaries of journal articles. It became clear that the instructor was consistently giving A's to summaries in which the student identified the problem that the article dealt with, paraphrased the article's solutions to that problem, and explained briefly how these solutions were related to his or her nursing career. Once the teacher clearly articulated the qualities she was looking for, it was possible for her to describe those qualities to her students.

Improving Students' Writing

Throughout this chapter, I have avoided discussion of such topics as spelling, usage, and sentence structure. Although many students need a good bit of help with these problems, they are not the only things instructors need to be concerned about when they consider students' writing. In other words, it is possible to use writing to help students understand the subject matter of a particular course, even if students have had little previous instruction in writing.

Of course, we must not assume that any one method or any one course will solve all the problems students have when they try to write. Students' habits and attitudes have developed over a number of years, and they will not magically change overnight. But each course can contribute to students' understanding of a basic part of the composing process—the part that entails thinking about and formulating one's understanding of a particular subject matter. As we improve students' ability to do this, we make an important contribution to their ability to write. At the same time, we get on with the business of teaching the subjects we were hired to teach in the first place.

References

Elbow, P. *Writing Without Teachers*. New York: Oxford University Press, 1975.
Sternberg, R. J. *Intelligence Applied*. San Diego: Harcourt Brace Jovanovich, 1986.
Young, R., Becker, A., and Pike, K. *Rhetoric: Discovery and Change*. San Diego: Harcourt Brace Jovanovich, 1970.

Lee Odell is professor of composition theory and research at Rensselaer Polytechnic Institute, where he is also director of graduate studies for the Department of Language, Literature, and Communication.

Traditional WAC practices need to be reevaluated in light of contemporary literacy problems in community colleges.

Toward a New Paradigm in Writing Across the Curriculum

Martin B. Spear, Dennis McGrath, Evan Seymour

The initiation of WAC programs in community colleges over the past decade has been of considerable significance. It has signaled the importance the academic community has begun to accord literacy instruction in the preparation of students, as well as the consequent need for faculty from all disciplines to consider the role of language in instruction. Thus, WAC is no longer just a bright idea. At community colleges, its practices have become mostly standardized. Advocates have very specific recommendations for assigning writing, which they routinely offer their colleagues, and very specific ideas about how writing advances literacy.

Now that this "first generation" of WAC has been standardized, there is a critical need to reassess the theory and practice of such programs, especially in light of the emerging recognition of literacy problems in community colleges. As recent research indicates, literacy standards have been weakened the most at these institutions, at the same time that the challenge of the academic preparation of nontraditional students is greatest (Richardson, Fisk, and Okun, 1983).

The work of Richardson, Fisk, and Okun is particularly interesting and valuable because, rather than focusing on the academic deficiencies of students entering the community college, these researchers consider how the academic culture of the open-access college has subtly changed, and how the practice and social meaning of literacy has gradually paled. Traditionally, Richardson and his colleagues argue, colleges insisted on "texting"— the use of reading and writing to comprehend or compose connected language as exhibited, for example, in extensive primary-source reading and frequent and varied essay writing. Open-access colleges, however, have undergone a pronounced shift toward "bitting"—the use of degraded forms of linguistic practice, in which students are cued to respond to or produce decontextualized, isolated, nonrhetorical and fragmented language. Typical "bitting" practices in the classroom find students reading textbooks rather than primary texts and writing (when they write at all) summaries and recapitulations or doing exercises in locating information and defining words. Evaluative practices now come down to tests of information retrieval, through the device of short-answer exams: true-and-false or fill-in-the-blanks items, as well as matching and multiple-choice questions. Since nontraditional students' hopes for academic advancement and career mobility depend heavily on their becoming much more sophisticated with language use, these findings are very unsettling.

The question that community colleges confront today is not whether writing is useful in instruction, or whether faculty collaboration should be encouraged, or whether writing should be pursued in a sustained way; all these questions have been settled by the success of the first generation of WAC programs. Rather, the important question now concerns how to use institutional writing programs to reconstruct and strengthen the academic environment of open-access institutions, so as to prepare nontraditional students better for further academic work and enhance their career mobility. Two major aspects of these programs need reassessment: their conceptualization of writing as a generic skill, and their reliance on the notion of writing as a learning tool.

Writing as a Generic Skill

Writing, in too many instances, has come to be understood as a generic skill, transportable to (and reinforceable in) any classroom in any discipline. This view of writing is increasingly criticized. Researchers and writing theorists studying the role of convention in the act of composing (Bartholomae, 1985; Reither, 1985), the social construction of knowledge (Bruffee, 1984), and the new sociology of science and the study of academic disciplines (Geertz, 1983; Bazerman, 1981; Kuhn, 1970) concur in emphasizing both the density and complexity of disciplinary knowledge and communication and the specificity of discourse conventions. Writing instruction, according to this view, should be designed to help students become initiated into disciplines understood as discourse communities, to become so-called knowledgeable peers who can demonstrate their competent membership by understanding and deploying the actual forms of argument, description, and explanation—the modes of knowing of that discipline.

Writing as a Learning Tool

First-generation WAC programs have advanced the notion of writing as integral to learning—as representing, in Emig's (1977, p. 122) terms, "a unique mode of learning." In advancing this view of writing as a mode of learning, initial WAC practices primarily drew theoretical support from individual learning theory and from cognitive psychology and so framed their appeal in terms of giving content teachers techniques for helping students learn better.

The basic problem, of course, is that writing is paradigmatically a social performance within a discourse community. Thus, WAC practices that depend entirely on individual learning processes are bound to be interpersonally irrelevant or, at best, impoverished. With respect to individual disciplines, which, after all, are the target for WAC, this means that if writing is really to count in the classroom, it must be because the intellectual structure of the classroom and the discipline demand it and because writing partly forms the intellectual structure of that classroom and that discipline. Insisting on a generic justification for writing leads to the detachment of reading and writing from the norms and practices of particular disciplines and groups of disciplines, in favor of global arguments focusing on proposed individual learning psychology. But detachment from actual writing communities allows only relatively impoverished forms and uses of writing (and, analogously, of reading), which rely heavily on solipsistic and expressivistic models. This situation leads, naturally, to practices emphasizing "private writing" and, later, to awkward and artificial attempts to integrate the student into a discipline-specific discourse community.

Setting aside everything that can be said in favor of such devices as ungraded and private free writing, journals, or learning logs, we need to acknowledge the impact of such practices on academic culture. The disciplines have conventions that constrain public discourse while showing absolutely no interest whatsoever in private, introspective, or ruminatory discourse. Unless one were generally committed to the problematic notion that the private is prior to the public, and that this is a feature not only of expressive writing but also of disciplinary learning and discourse, then one would feel little compulsion to insist so strongly on the universal merit of the private jotting down of reactions. One is bound to note that the rigorous frameworks and standards of disputation and discourse within the disciplines are certain to be mysterious and threatening to neophytes. To hope for a royal road around these obstacles, however, is simply to debase or misrepresent the nature of rational discourse and the educational challenge we face in initiating nontraditional students into academic life.

Toward a New Paradigm: Writing Within a Curriculum

Community College of Philadelphia's (CCP) Transfer Opportunities Program (TOP) brings together groups of thirty full-time students with teams of four faculty members from one of two broad academic areas, social sciences or the humanities, and provides those students with one twelve-credit course of study per semester in one of those two areas. Students who test into college-level writing courses, who indicate an interest in transferring to a four-year college, and who do not choose one of CCP's career curricula are invited into TOP. About ninety students per semester accept that invitation. Writing instruction in TOP is the responsibility of all four team members. On the humanities team, for example, there is one teacher of art history, one teacher of literature, one teacher of philosophy, and one teacher of social and political history.

An important context for writing instruction is the agreed-on set of practices that constitutes the program itself. These practices were originally agreed to in a long series of discussions among TOP faculty and teams between 1983 and 1987. For example, there is regular team consultation on all aspects of the program. All writing assignments and examinations are designed, administered, and read by the team. There is a series of lectures that are at least roughly coordinated, and two weekly two-hour seminars engage students in close readings of primary and secondary texts (including the texts of the questions that constitute the midsemester and final examinations). Midsemester conferences are held with all students. There are also writing practices, described in the sections that follow. Briefly, what the faculty intends to give students through such practices is initial immersion in the culture of academic social science for one semester and in academic humanities for another.

Only two or three major writing assignments are given per semester, and the creation of these assignments necessitates many hours of writing, discussing, and rewriting on the part of the faculty team. The resulting assignments are difficult to understand—difficult, in a sense, for faculty as well as for students, since they focus on real and complex problems that are still subjects of debate in academic circles and in the wider intellectual world.

The sequence of writing activities that follows the faculty team's creation of a writing assignment spreads over a month or longer. (The faculty text is termed a "call for papers" by the current humanities team to distinguish it from responses and to place it and students' responses within serious academic discourse.) The call is passed out to students and discussed in one or two full-size class sessions, called "large writing groups." In such sessions, the faculty do not explain what the call "really means" but instead press students to give readings of phrases, sentences, and groups of sentences in the call, with special attention to the relations between these various parts. ("That second sentence—does it seem to provide an extension of the claim made in the first? An exception? A qualification? Does it open up a path of exploration? Close one off? Provide a kind of caution? 'If you go down this path, keep in mind. . . .' ") In other words, this faculty text is treated in the same way that other primary and secondary texts are treated in the program. What students find most difficult to accept—as do faculty who have long been immersed in community college culture—is the idea that students' texts should be treated as seriously and in the same manner as texts by Nietzsche or Dickens.

That seriousness and manner can be described in this way: After about a week, the first public version of the paper (typed, double spaced, two to four pages) is due in each student's "small writing group," one copy for each of the eight students and one for the faculty member in the group. At the beginning of the small-writing-group session itself, someone who is not the author of the paper (often the teacher) reads the paper aloud, faithfully following the spelling and punctuation that appears on the page. After a pause of a minute or so, the teacher asks the group to characterize some aspect of the paper. Characterizing a text, describing what actually is on the page, is not an easy task, and often students stray off into traditional composition-teacher tasks, such as talking about what is *not* on the page ("not enough examples") and what should be there ("it needs an introduction"). Thus, the TOP writing-group teacher is kept busy turning the conversation back to the description of various rhetorical events that are actually occurring on the page, asking the student the same kinds of questions that are asked of every text in the course.

Persuading students, through the dynamics of writing-group interactions, that their texts should be taken as seriously as any other texts is difficult, but almost every student makes significant strides during the semester toward just this kind of seriousness about his or her own and other students' writings. A writing-group conversation of this kind, even on a paragraph or two of a student's paper, often takes up a full one-hour session.

Throughout the session, the author remains silent. The author's text does the talking, and so the author is not forced into either defending what the text says or wandering down that endless road of intentions: "What I really meant to say there was . . . ." Because the author gets to see just how his or her paper is being read or even misread, he or she gains the opportunity to make changes that can encourage some readings and discourage others.

Writing groups, perhaps surprisingly, are not set up primarily to help the author whose paper is being read. Rather, a writing-group session is primarily an activity that brings its members into the regular practice of talking about language, about the distinction between saying one thing and saying something that sounds almost the same, a distinction that usually has little importance in the discourse communities from which students are drawn but is the lifeblood of the academic and professional discourse communities into which they are being initiated. As students become more and more proficient at standing back from a text and describing what is going on in it, they become more and more capable of doing the same with their own texts. In other words, students are led to learn how to *write* their own papers by being led to learn how to *read* them.

The small writing groups meet once or twice per week during the month or longer when second and third (usually final) public versions are produced. The benefits of writing groups are seen by faculty as flowing primarily to the circle of students struggling to comment meaningfully on the paper at hand.

The end of the process is anticlimactic: one or two faculty members, neither of whom was the student's writing-group leader, read a student's paper, describe it to the student in a handwritten note of about a page, assign a grade, and return it. By then, it is old news. By then, the student, his or her peers, and his or her writing-group leader all know where the paper has been, where it is headed, and just how far it went before the artificial imposition of the due date. By then, too, another call for papers has been issued.

Conclusion

The next generation of WAC, if it is to confront the central problem of open-access institutions—the paling of literacy standards and the weakening of disciplines—must assume a sympathetic but critical stance toward earlier practices. Initial efforts to emphasize the importance of language use in the intellectual preparation of students, and to draw all faculty into sustained and consistent work with writing, must be continued. Nevertheless, these practices must be closely scrutinized and judged in terms of their capacity to revitalize institutional literacy standards. Writing programs must be designed to help disciplinary faculty identify for themselves the characteristic forms of thought and the conventions and styles of their fields, so that they can develop pedagogical practices that enact those understandings in the classroom. Students' initiation into the academic and disciplinary discourse community demands their own engagement with that community, however alien, subtle, and complex it may appear to them. It cannot be imagined that their early efforts will be strikingly successful; the process of initiation is bound to be difficult and, in some ways, painful. But, again, there is no royal road. There is no way but the hard way.

References

Bartholomae, D. "Inventing the University." In M. Rose (ed.), When a Writer Can't Write. New York: Guilford Press, 1985.

Bazerman, C. "What Written Knowledge Does: Three Examples of Academic Discourse." Philosophy of the Social Sciences, 1981, 11, 361–387.

Bruffee, K. A. "Collaborative Writing and the Conversation of Mankind." College English, 1984, 46 (7), 635–652.

Emig, J. "Writing as a Mode of Learning." College Composition and Communication, 1977, 28 (2), 122–128.

Geertz, C. "The Way We Think Now: Toward an Ethnography of Modern Thought." In C. Geertz (ed.), Local Knowledge: Further Essays in Interpretive Anthropology. New York: Basic Books, 1983.

Kuhn, T. *The Structure of Scientific Revolutions.* (2nd ed.) Chicago: University of Chicago Press, 1970.

Reither, J. A. "Writing and Knowing: Toward Redefining the Writing Process." *College English*, 1985, 47 (6), 620–628.

Richardson, R. C., Jr., Fisk, E. C., and Okun, M. A. *Literacy in the Open-Access College.* San Francisco: Jossey-Bass, 1983.

Martin B. Spear is professor of philosophy at the Community College of Philadelphia.

Dennis McGrath is professor of sociology at the Community College of Philadelphia.

Evan Seymour is associate professor of English at the Community College of Philadelphia. He codirected the writing project of the Transfer Opportunities Program during its sponsorship by the Ford Foundation and is now a member of the program's Humanities Semester faculty.

Two geographically diverse WAC programs succeed in staff development because of good design and consistent administrative support.

A Solution to Student-Faculty Mismatch

Marsha Z. Cummins, Jacqueline Stuchin-Paprin, Judith R. Lambert

This chapter reflects two differing perspectives on the need for WAC programs at two diverse institutions. The first, Bronx Community College, a unit of the City University of New York (CUNY), in a poor inner-city neighborhood, is experiencing an extreme mismatch between the faculty's training and expectations and the students' ability to perform. The second, Richland College, part of the Dallas County Community College District (DCCCD), is in a suburban setting, and its students are less educationally disadvantaged. Despite these key differences, however, both institutions recognize the imperative for faculty development in responding to an educational environment that is changing for all community colleges.

Mismatch at Bronx Community College

At Bronx Community College, a mismatch exists between the faculty and the students, in terms of expectations, motivations, backgrounds, ethnicity, culture, and cognitive styles. On the one hand, the faculty member, as at all other CUNY branches, is expected to earn a doctoral degree and to publish, in order to achieve tenure and promotion. On the other hand, the faculty member faces the daunting challenge of severely underprepared students. In the sections that follow, we examine more fully some aspects of such mismatching, and then we present one institution's response to the problem.

Mismatched Faculty-Student Profiles. Coming from the poorest area of New York City, Bronx Community College students are overwhelmingly female and minority, and nearly half are not native English speakers. More than 90 percent require some basic-skills work in language arts and math-

NEW DIRECTIONS FOR COMMUNITY COLLEGES, no. 73, Spring 1991 © Jossey-Bass Inc., Publishers

ematics. The faculty, by contrast, is predominantly white and male, with a median age of fifty-two. Because of the reward system, a substantial number of faculty members are involved in scholarly research and publishing. As a result, Bronx faculty share with other community college teachers what Seidman (1985, p. 257) describes as an ambivalence toward the dual role of pursuing traditional scholarship and teaching in a community college.

Disparity in Cognitive Style. A critical dissimilarity between faculty and students shows up in the process of teaching and learning. Specifically, the cognitive style of the students can be viewed as what Cross (1976, pp. 111–133) calls "field-dependent." This suggests that the students have weak analytical and critical-thinking skills and are unaccustomed to independent thinking and autonomous action in an academic context. Most function best in a learning environment where there are opportunities for social interaction. Conversely, college instructors tend to be field-independent, structuring their pedagogy for learners who have a cognitive style similar to their own.

Faculty Attitudes. The faculty at Bronx, similar to those in Seidman's (1985) study, have exhibited negative responses to their role as educators, responses characterized by the resistance to learning more about their students and about what they as faculty can do to improve classroom instruction. Many have lowered their standards, assuming that the students are incapable of learning. Furthermore, most contend that basic-skills work has no legitimacy in a discipline-based classroom.

Solution to the Mismatch: The STARS Program. In 1980, Bronx began planning a staff development program to improve students' reading, writing, speaking, and listening skills. The dean of academic affairs appointed a faculty member to assist him in coordinating these efforts and then circulated a questionnaire to every department to elicit information on the levels of reading, writing, and speaking proficiency required for successful completion of each course. The results of the questionnaire demonstrated discrepancies between the levels of achievement that could reasonably be expected after one or two semesters of basic-skills courses and the levels of achievement required for success in various subjects. It was evident that follow-up or postremedial experiences were needed to bridge the gap.

With a federally funded Title III grant, Bronx initiated an ambitious staff development program designed to ameliorate this situation. It was called Strategies for Teaching and Reinforcing Skills (STARS). STARS was adapted from a model program (see Chapter Twelve) that immerses students in reading, writing, and speaking in content courses. STARS was divided into two phases. In the teaching phase, participating freshmen are given block schedules of courses that offer an overlapping, integrated curriculum in language development. In the second, or reinforcement, phase, content-area faculty implement a holistic language approach to learning.

The STARS Program has been in effect at Bronx for the past eight years, despite the cessation of federal funding in 1982. Its success can be attributed to definitive elements of its design. Along with institutional commitment, the inclusion of interdisciplinary/interdepartmental involvement, small-group work, weekly meetings, external rewards, voluntary commitment, and follow-up activities has been essential.

Reading, writing, and speaking courses were traditionally considered separate curricula at Bronx, under the direction of three different departments. Through the teaching phase, however, STARS integrates the skills curricula. Consequently, faculty who teach language-skills courses must plan cooperatively. In the reinforcement phase, faculty from diverse disciplines meet in groups of four with a trainer-facilitator, who guides them in their implementation of language skills within their content areas.

The small-group work provides a means of problem solving in a supportive atmosphere. Risk taking is encouraged, and success is recognized.

The length of the weekly meetings has varied from one to two hours. Nevertheless, the allocation of a specific time and day on a weekly basis creates continuity.

Although the STARS program is intrinsically motivational in its design, it also provides external rewards for participants. From half an hour to three hours of released time per semester have been given to faculty members according to the financial capacity of the institution and the extent of individual involvement. Instructors now receive half an hour of release time for the one-hour weekly meeting. Reinforcement trainers and trainees receive four hours for two semesters.

Participation in a program that requires the individual's virtual metamorphosis must be voluntary. Some faculty members have been attracted to the program by its offer of release time, but most participants have joined because of their genuine interest in improving students' academic competence. Given its voluntary nature, the STARS program is enthusiastically supported by the people involved. Follow-up has been established through systematic meeting times, periodic distribution of a newsletter, and semiannual luncheon meetings. Thus, through the dynamic interplay of institutional commitment, environments responsive to students' learning needs, and program design, Bronx Community College has developed a program that ameliorates the mismatch between students and faculty.

The Essential Role of the Richland College Administration

Mismatch between faculty and students in the Dallas County Community College District is less extreme than at Bronx because research and publication play no part in the faculty reward system. Even though good teaching is their primary goal, however, Richland College faculty still struggle with the change that has occurred over the past twenty years in students' academic preparation and attitudes. Hence, faculty development programs fulfill an important need on DCCCD's campuses, too.

Because most DCCCD faculty are student-centered, they are receptive to strategies that enhance students' success. Nevertheless, WAC has flourished on some campuses and floundered on others, even when careful planning, voluntary participation, small-group work, and follow-up were present (as in the Bronx program). The essential element of success or failure in the DCCCD programs has been the role of the college administration. The remainder of this chapter describes the administrative aspects necessary to the fostering of a healthy WAC program: clear expectations, unflagging support, adequate time, and money.

Expectations. An explicit statement of tasks, timelines, parameters, and available funds constitutes the first ingredient of a successful WAC program. At Richland College, the administration, drawing on models of managerial excellence (Peters and Waterman, 1982), sets goals and solves problems collaboratively with the faculty, allowing time for participatory management. Thus, with release time for an entire academic year, an interdisciplinary committee studied WAC programs, assessed needs, focused on specific goals, and developed a written plan appropriate to the Richland campus.

A necessary corollary to clear expectations is a written proposal that articulates goals and clarifies assumptions about writing and about students. With this proposal, the administrators and the faculty responsible for the program have an additional opportunity to eliminate ambiguity.

With clear goals and expectations established by administrators and WAC leaders, faculty can participate with the assurance that they are investing in something that administrators value. Specifically, their participation in this program is recognized and rewarded in their evaluations.

Administrative Support. Clear expectations and goals lead to but do not ensure a second necessary element: continual and visible support for the program. If a WAC program flares brilliantly and then fizzles, the problem may be the changing priorities of the leaders or of new administrators and the lack of visible and audible support. Pressured by the public, by students who want credits and degrees, and by budgets that constrict, administrators may not demonstrate consistent support. Since the Richland plan, like others in the Dallas system, relies on voluntary participation, the WAC program needed a strong and consistent message from the top. Fortunately, Richland College's president had solicited the concerns of faculty members in proposing ten priorities for the college in its second decade. To publicize these priorities, he wrote a series of articles, including one on WAC, for the weekly campus newsletter. Another example of visible administrative support on the Richland campus is the focus on the WAC program at an annual faculty convocation at the beginning of each academic year. At this event, WAC is featured in slides and videotapes, and small discussion groups are led by enthusiastic WAC participants from various disciplines. The president, the vice-president of instruction, and the division chairs also attend WAC workshops. Here, they learn about the subtleties and complexities of writing. In this way, administrators model the participation required of faculty members and encourage reluctant faculty to attend these workshops.

Time and Money. Administrators must provide two other elements for a program to succeed—time and money. Fundamental changes in pedagogy occur gradually. Faculty need more than a year or two of workshops to integrate and sustain a process approach to writing in their classes. Thus, long-term institutional commitment is crucial to the encouragement of faculty's commitment because pedagogical change is unwieldy and often discomfiting. When the rewards are intrinsic, that is, when faculty participate without stipends or release time, faculty need to know that the institution is also committed. DCCCD faculty, who teach five classes each semester (some add one or two for extra service), must carve out time to attend WAC workshops and implement writing strategies. Although most are committed to improving the learning environment in their classrooms, some become discouraged when rewards are not forthcoming in the form of tenure or promotion.

Even if external funds are used to establish a WAC program, college funds will be needed at some point to sustain it. With shrinking budgets, administrators must be apprised of long-term expenditures before an initial commitment. Again, a written plan can make these needs clear to administrators and allow faculty leaders to know what they can depend on.

We hope that administrators and program planners alike will find our experiences and perspectives helpful. Regardless of institutional setting, certain process elements are essential to a successful faculty development program: interdisciplinary collaboration, regular and frequent small-group meetings among participating faculty, voluntary commitment, and rewards for participation. Even when these elements exist, a WAC staff development program still needs a supportive administration.

References

Cross, K. P. *Accent on Learning.* San Francisco: Jossey-Bass, 1976.

Peters, T., and Waterman, R., Jr. *In Search of Excellence: Lessons from America's Best-Run Companies.* New York: Harper & Row, 1982.

Seidman, E. *In the Words of the Faculty: Perspectives on Improving Teaching and Educational Quality in Community Colleges.* San Francisco: Jossey-Bass, 1985.

Marsha Z. Cummins is a member of the English department and writing coordinator at Bronx Community College. She also directs the WAC program.

Jacqueline Stuchin-Paprin is chair of the Department of Special Education Services at Bronx Community College. She was formerly assistant to the dean of academic affairs, with responsibility for staff development on campus.

Judith R. Lambert teaches freshman composition and interdisciplinary team-taught Humanities and English courses in the honors program at Richland College, where she developed and now directs the WAC program.

Given diverse college needs and resources, WAC workshops vary widely in style and complexity, but planners can profit by following certain guidelines.

The WAC Workshop

Julie Bertch, Delryn R. Fleming

The advertising-art instructor said that students must be able to describe their ideas in writing before they ever draw a line. The automotive instructor agreed: performance-based classes must incorporate writing skills. His students intend to become customer-service managers, who have to justify claims in writing or lose thousands of dollars per year. The chemistry instructor shared a technique that the nursing instructor could use in class, while the ESL teacher and the math teacher collaborated on an assignment that would help students in both classes clarify their thinking. The setting for all this activity? A WAC workshop.

Occasional tips in a faculty newsletter and sharing of journal articles are helpful, but the most popular and comprehensive way of introducing colleagues to the theories and methods of Writing Across the Curriculum has become the WAC workshop. Although the differing needs and resources of various community colleges have resulted in many kinds of workshops, certain guidelines have emerged that offer important information for planners. These suggestions involve participants' roles, workshop content and environment, and follow-up activities.

Participants' Roles

The most effective WAC workshops come about in response to faculty's needs. Regardless of how ardently administrators or WAC directors believe in the value of using writing in all courses, faculty must come to the workshop setting voluntarily and with the expectation of finding something useful. They may be hesitant—they may be facing a five-course load with large classes and feel that adding writing assignments to their courses

NEW DIRECTIONS FOR COMMUNITY COLLEGES, no. 73, Spring 1991 © Jossey-Bass Inc., Publishers

would require a time commitment they cannot afford to make. They may also have concerns about what they can expect from writing assignments, as well as doubts about their ability to grade such assignments. For some, the issue is complicated by their already having tried writing assignments that failed.

Still, many faculty continue to think of writing as a valuable tool for thinking and as a necessary job skill for students. Planners need to build on that perception by providing campuswide information on a regular basis to create a receptive audience before holding a workshop. They also need to provide incentives that will encourage faculty to spend valuable time attending a workshop. Moreover, in an environment where tenure or extra pay may not be connected to staff development, planners need to find other ways to confer professional recognition. Top administrators can signal strong support by financing workshop costs and attending some of the sessions. Campus leadership councils can endorse a WAC movement as a valuable service to students and the teaching profession. Participation in regular workshops throughout the academic year can substitute for committee assignments.

Recruiting Participants

The primary task of any WAC workshop is to convince faculty of the need for and value of writing in their courses. They need to believe that every student can become an adequate writer who can use writing to achieve his or her purposes, and that all students can develop enough skill in writing to make noticeable improvements in their college work and in their confidence as students. Faculty also need to see WAC as a collegewide priority.

The success of any workshop, whether it runs for four hours or two days or two weeks, will depend on the commitment it develops among its participants. The most promising outcomes begin with faculty who value writing and are willing to invest their time and effort in making writing a route to improved learning. A few people will hear about a workshop and ask to come, but others need more specific recruitment. If interest in improving students' writing begins with a core group of knowledgeable and enthusiastic teachers, they need only persuade their colleagues to join a purposeful campus effort. If the group is smaller (perhaps only a single staff development coordinator, or a newly appointed WAC director), the task will require more time to be spent on disseminating information and recruiting. Participants must know enough about WAC to choose to attend. They may have some reservations, and they may feel unsure about their commitment to writing, but they must come voluntarily. A workshop leader will have a difficult time dealing with the anxieties and negative attitudes brought by coerced participants.

Attracting good people, who will actively participate in the workshop and effectively implement writing activities in their classes, requires personal contact. The teaching fields of faculty recruiters are not important, but their relationships with other faculty are. Their connections are the key, along with their ability to convince their peers that using writing in the teaching/learning process will improve students' performance in measurable ways. Writing makes real contributions to learning, and all instructors can teach their students a few effective writing-for-learning strategies, without sacrificing significant content in an already full syllabus.

Logistics

Workshop planners must consider certain logistical problems. Decisions about location and scheduling of the workshop are critical. For a workshop scheduled during the school year, meetings off campus—completely removed from offices, telephones, messages, and students—will let participants focus solely on writing and learning. Even when a workshop is scheduled outside the school year, an environment that is free of familiar distractions is preferable. The workshop requires participants' undivided attention if it is to accomplish its essential goals: creating an opportunity for teachers to learn about the purposes and techniques of using writing in their disciplines, discovering what their colleagues across the country are saying about their experiences with WAC, and discussing these ideas among themselves. A new environment, separate from the typical school experience, also allows participants to interact in different ways and establish new alignments in cross-disciplinary relationships. A hotel meeting room may be ideal for presentations because it is no one's turf; the university library may be the best place for discovering new resources because it belongs to everyone.

A college calendar does not provide the perfect meeting time. Some colleges hold longer workshops during the summer, giving participants time to examine the literature in their disciplines and share new ideas. An intensive two-week project, such as the one conducted by the Maricopa County Community College District, in Phoenix, Arizona, allows faculty the time they need to become comfortable with their roles in assigning and coaching student writing. This longer workshop also encourages participants to become committed to the long-term objectives of a collegewide writing program. Those who favor this type of workshop are convinced that periods of uninterrupted, unpressured time for participants to think, talk, and plan are essential.

Other colleges find the intensive workshop neither possible nor necessary. They may choose to hold two-day workshops or schedule shorter sessions during the semester. While workshops may be as brief as three hours, most planners agree that two days is the minimum time needed to effect significant changes in instruction. Brookhaven College of the Dallas County Community College District has tried a "reinforcement" series of short workshops over a two-year period, with the same participants and facilitator attending each session. As the faculty grow in understanding of and experience with the methods tried, they begin to dictate the content of the workshops.

The choice of a facilitator may be the most important decision to be made. Good workshop leaders must be experienced, supportive, enthusiastic, and able to establish credibility quickly with the workshop participants. The old maxim about an expert's having to come from over fifty miles away may hold true, but not necessarily. After two or three "expertly" conducted workshops, Richland College (Dallas) had great success with inside facilitators—faculty who had been to workshops and tried methods that worked and who wanted to share what they had learned. The Maricopa Colleges had equally positive results with local people, whose interest in the writing-for-learning movement had led them to develop expertise in the field and share it with their colleagues.

The best suggestions for workshop facilitators probably come from personal recommendations. As more faculty develop successful techniques, make presentations at conferences, and write about them in journals, the number of able and available workshop leaders grows. The best practice is to consult the network—to read about and write to or call people whose work looks interesting and ask for their advice.

Planning the Content

The content of a workshop may vary widely according to the style and experience of the facilitator and the requests of the planners. Certain important concepts should be covered, however. The theoretical basis of the writing-for-learning movement—that writing is a way of thinking—is primary. This approach describes the similarities between writing and learning as writing becomes a way of discovering and knowing. Participants consider and respond to three premises: that more learning is achieved when writing activities are included in the learning situation, that learning to write is not just learning grammar and spelling but also learning to think in the language and strategies of a discipline, and that writing can help students become actively connected with the content of any course. In doing so, participants acquire a sense of the perspective that underlies the whole WAC movement.

Since the nature of the interaction between writing and thinking is seen as the critical factor for learning, participants should be encouraged to design assignments that will produce appropriate thinking (Wolfe and Pope, 1985). If teachers can identify the thinking activities that their more successful students use, they can design writing activities that will pattern these more effective thinking processes for the less successful students. Repeated opportunities to practice the skills that these activities require will enhance students' likelihood of (and expectations for) success.

The idea that writing is a process is also fundamental. Assignments that allow for planning and revision are best for teaching any content. For example, the value of informal strategies, such as reflective writing, becomes clearer when students have several opportunities to write reflectively and to note their own progress. Students need to understand that learning involves stages of growth and that neither their instructors' nor their own expectations are likely to be met in a first draft. Emphasis on the process will also encourage the view of learning as a connected, ongoing experience with content rather than a process of collecting information for a test.

The organization of the workshop should allow participants to develop some immediately useful ideas and materials. Individual and group projects alike can be useful in helping participants plan for their own courses. Initial group activities can emphasize appropriate goals and identify constraints by asking teachers to articulate (in writing) their assumptions about how students learn content material. Next, asking them to specify the kinds of knowledge and insights that students can learn best through writing will provide a useful base for developing assignments. Finally, if individual participants are asked to describe the actual demands that their courses make on students, they can realistically evaluate whether their expectations are appropriate (and whether they need to adjust them to students' abilities). At this point, attention is closely focused on what students are doing and achieving in their courses.

In searching for what works, faculty can find a wealth of ideas in current WAC literature (Maimon and others, 1981; Wolfe and Pope, 1985). Short, in-class, ungraded writing may be a good starting place for faculty new to writing assignments. Asking students to reflect in writing before a discussion not only aids discussion content but also improves class participation (Middleman and Blaylock, 1983; Morrissey, 1982). Assigning a summary of lecture notes to be used as notes for a test gives students an incentive to write. A memo to the instructor or journal-writing assignments open dialogue with students on content, without the necessity of the instructor's assigning a grade (Knoblauch and Brannon, 1983; Fulwiler, 1979). More organized summaries of chapters (Lambert, 1984; Nickel, 1985) or summaries written as "microthemes" on index cards (Bean, Drenk, and Lee, 1982) require students to think clearly before they write. Collaborative writing assignments have the potential of teaching more content than students may learn alone (Moss and Holder, 1988). Students also learn about the value of teamwork, differences in writing styles, and the need for revision. Once the concept of writing to learn becomes familiar to them, faculty participants readily generate suggestions such as these for their own content areas.

As a small-group project, participants can select a few writing-to-learn strategies and design a generic method or format for presenting them to their students. An important element of this activity is noting and discussing the adaptations that particular disciplines may require. This element is important for the emphasis it places on teaching and learning and the opportunity it provides for interdisciplinary sharing and understanding. Finally, each participant needs to develop an individual plan for integrating chosen strategies into his or her courses, deciding when and where to present, cue, and reinforce their use. Each instructor should leave the workshop with a clear plan for using writing and the enthusiasm to make it work.

Follow-Up Activities

Follow-up is essential. To ensure continued success, participants need to meet regularly and report their progress, share their successes, analyze attempts that did not work, and discuss their plans. These meetings can expand the faculty development aspect of the program by featuring outside speakers as well as participants' presentations, providing ongoing opportunities to learn about what helps students learn, and encouraging innovative ideas. Both the number and the complexity of writing assignments will increase as faculty discover and invent techniques for using writing and give their colleagues the benefit of their experience.

Planners of follow-up programs should also encourage teachers themselves to write—to know the satisfaction, the renewal, and the commitment to writing that accompany the writing experience, as well as to experience the struggles and frustrations that students face. Faculty who write will benefit themselves, their students, their colleges, and their disciplines.

Changing the existing situation and improving the quality of writing and learning among our students will require us to enlist the talents of the faculty and the support of the administration—in depth and over the long term. We have to raise awareness of the problem throughout the campus, making it clear that students' writing deficiencies hinder their progress in both academic and occupational programs and that ignoring the situation worsens it. We need to present workshops that result in specific, purposeful efforts by faculty to understand the writing/learning connection, to identify essential writing strategies, and to develop ways to integrate writing into their courses in effective ways. To achieve these aims, faculty must be supported in strong, practical programs that encourage their participation and growth. Teachers who have the opportunity to articulate their concerns about students' learning, unify their goals and purposes for instruction, and incorporate writing in their courses, through theoretically sound and well-planned methods, will see results that give us all a renewed optimism about excellence.

References

Bean, J. C., Drenk, D., and Lee, F. D. "Microtheme Strategies for Developing Cognitive Skills." In C. W. Griffin (ed.), *Teaching Writing in All Disciplines*. New Directions for Teaching and Learning, no. 12. San Francisco: Jossey-Bass, 1982.

Fulwiler, T. "Journal Writing Across the Curriculum." In G. Stanford (ed.), *How to Handle the Paper Load.* Urbana, Ill.: National Council of Teachers of English, 1979.

Knoblauch, C. H., and Brannon, L. "Writing as Learning Through the Curriculum." *College English,* 1983, 45 (5), 465–474.

Lambert, J. R. "Summaries: A Focus for Basic Writers." *Journal of Developmental Education,* 1984, 8 (2), 10–12, 32.

Maimon, E., Belcher, G., Hearn, G. W., Nodine, B. F., and O'Connor, F. W. *Writing in the Arts and Sciences.* Cambridge, Mass.: Winthrop, 1981.

Middleman, L. I., and Blaylock, B. K. "Writing = Learning: Building Quantitative Skills Through Writing." *Collegiate News and Views,* 1983, 37 (1), 7–10.

Morrissey, T. J. "The Five-Minute Entry: A Writing Exercise for Large Classes in All Disciplines." *Exercise Exchange,* 1982, 27 (1), 41–42.

Moss, A., and Holder, C. "Assigning Writing." In *Improving Student Writing: A Guidebook for Faculty in All Disciplines.* Dubuque, Iowa: Kendall/Hunt, 1988.

Nickel, D. A. "An Alternative to Midterm Exams." *Innovation Abstracts,* 1985, 7 (10).

Wolfe, D., and Pope, C. "Developing Thinking Processes: Ten Writing-for-Learning Tasks Throughout the Curriculum." *Virginia English Bulletin: What We Know About the Teaching of Writing,* 1985, 35 (1), 11–17.

Julie Bertch is a faculty member at Rio Salado Community College in Phoenix, Arizona, and director of the Maricopa Writing Project.

Delryn R. Fleming is a faculty member at Brookhaven College in Dallas, Texas, and serves as Writing Across the Curriculum director.

The journal and the microtheme, two versatile writing-to-learn strategies, are easily adapted to math, biology, electrical technology, and college-life courses.

Writing-to-Learn Assignments: The Journal and the Microtheme

Linda C. Stanley

Because WAC programs are for the most part interdisciplinary, writing assignments that can be adapted to any subject are those most often introduced and utilized. Primary among these generic approaches to writing are the *journal* and the *microtheme*. While the microtheme most nearly resembles traditional academic writing assignments, the journal reflects students' more immediate connections to subject matter, which include their personal reactions, as well as more intellectual ruminations or speculations. Both assignments are used to encourage students to think about the subject matter and therefore to enhance their thinking and learning.

These generic assignments have been particularly useful for stressing writing in such disciplines as math, which often do not conceive of writing as having a place in their curricula and therefore have not developed discourse-centered assignments. These assignments are also helpful in departments that, for various reasons, have ceased to assign writing. The sciences and technologies, for example, often dispense with the narrative sections of lab reports and with essays on examinations. In our WRIT (Writing and Reading in the Technologies) Project at Queensborough Community College, we have successfully utilized both these strategies across the curriculum—in biology, mathematics, electrical and computer-engineering technology, and in an introduction to college life course taught by our counseling department.

The Journal

Ambron (1987, pp. 263–64) relates how and why she utilized the journal in an introductory cell-biology course: "One of the first strategies I employ is the use of student journals. As described by Toby Fulwiler, a journal is a cross between a student notebook and a writer's diary. The student records both information and a personal reaction to it. Journal-keeping, unlike passive notetaking, actively engages students in the course content.

"Setting aside 5 minutes of each 50-minute lecture period to write in a journal provides a limbering-up exercise to get students writing. I vary the time and focus of journal entries to increase their awareness of the value of writing, both personally and academically."

On Monday, she may ask students to write whatever is on their minds that may interfere with their concentration. After a test, they record their reactions to the grade. In addition to encouraging them to chronicle their emotional states, Ambron also suggests that they summarize what they have learned in class: "Today in my biology class I came in with a clear mind even though it's looking lousy outside. The three important things which I think are important and that I learned are: (1) the different types of bonds, (2) the result of their chemical reactions, and (3) different amounts of potential energy each has" (p. 264). At the end of class, she may ask students to summarize the lecture, as if responding to another student who has missed it and wants to know what happened in class: "Yo man we just talked membranes. Yo did you know that they were dynamic; that mean they are active. Yo what are you stupid. That mean like when they are hungry they engulf food, part of the external membrane becomes the internal because it forms a vacuole. Yo man it fresh when you think about it" (p. 264).

According to Svitak (personal communication, August 3, 1988), "Journal questions aid students to create their own resourcebooks because they a) present 'coming attractions,' b) keep track of concepts that will be extended, c) draw attention to key notions, d) prepare review before and after exams, and e) allow students to record personal reactions." For example, before lessons in her math classes on the first derivative, Svitak uses journal questions to direct students' attention to upcoming related concepts, such as extreme points and continuity, and to instruct students to review the tangent function, so that only a few minutes in class are needed to refresh their memories. Afterward, students describe in their journals what the first derivative means in geometrical terms.

In a freshman orientation class, Papier also assigns a journal. The class, a four-week seminar, is an attempt to help students understand entry into college as a turning point in their lives and realize that their college careers will include challenging intellectual, vocational, emotional, physical, and social growth. Papier (1988) considers writing an effective tool for promoting introspection and students' self-development process. She quotes Rennert (1973, p. 106) whose students "moved off dead center and were stimulated to discover, through writing, knowledge about their values and attitudes."

Each orientation session ends with a journal exercise. The question at the end of the first session is "Who am I?" In other sessions, students are asked to discuss the most important people in their lives and to answer the question "Who do I want to be, and how do I decide this?" Of students' responses, Papier (1988) concludes, "The important thing is that regardless of their grammar and syntax—correct or less so—most students in their writing express themselves freely and openly. They describe the common denominators of excessive work loads, parenting while they are in school, romantic concerns, and, almost universally, a desire to succeed in school."

The Microtheme

The microtheme is an essay so short that it can be typed on a single five-by-eight-inch notecard. Unlike the journal, the microtheme deemphasizes individuality and creativity, forcing students to concentrate on technique. Like the journal, the microtheme is a writing-to-learn strategy, since students must engage in considerable concentration before they can decide what is important to record. Bean, Drenk, and Lee (1982) have devised several types of microthemes: the summary-posing microtheme, the thesis-support microtheme, the data-provided microtheme, and the quandary-posing microtheme. Ambron (1987, p. 265) finds the data-provided microtheme helpful in improving students' inductive powers. She gives this twofold data-provided microtheme assignment to her cell-biology class:

1. Using the data supplied, graph the results of the three different experiments, using a different symbol for each. Provide the reader with a key and calculate the rate for each trial.
2. Write a paragraph discussing the experimental results. Include answers to the following questions: What conclusions can you make about pH and enzyme activity? Why does pH have an effect on enzyme activity? What is the optimum pH of this enzyme? Where would you expect this enzyme to function in your body?

She adds that the quandary-posing microtheme is the most enjoyable to design and the most fun for students to answer. Here is an example (p. 266).

> Dear Abby,
>   My wife and I have been under great stress, which I fear may lead to divorce. Our problem is this: On September 12 my wife gave birth to a 7lb, 8oz boy. His blood type is O-positive. My blood type is A-negative, and my wife's blood type is B-positive. I was never a good science student and would like to know if I could be the father. Please ask your experts and let me know as soon as possible.
>
>   Confused

Your task is to write an answer to Mr. Confused about the genetics of the ABO blood groups and Rh factor. Using all combinations possible, explain whether or not he could be the biological father of the O-positive baby.

Svitak (personal communication, August 3, 1988) believes that the journal and the microtheme are a "dynamic duo" that help all students become the active learners that they must be to master math skills. She has students write five microthemes over the semester. By requiring one or more drafts, she is able to interact individually with her students. Microthemes alone or with journal questions help students analyze problem-solving techniques; synthesize, compare, and contrast ideas; show applications to various fields; gain more from tightly packed courses; distinguish between a principal idea and its supporting details; organize or summarize the main ideas of one or more lessons; and conjecture about theorems. Svitak concludes:

In finite math or probability, after a series of journal questions about specific applications of counting procedures, students explain in microthemes when and where to use tree diagrams, Venn diagrams, etc. Or, in algebra, students describe the key idea that allows a complex fraction to be written in the form a+bj and show by example how to actually do it. Tech students might examine how they use complex numbers to represent alternating current circuits. In calculus, students can ponder in writing whether or not continuous functions have derivatives defined everywhere and, if not, produce a counter-example. Perhaps some students will even consider the converse question and conjecture a synthesis of both into a theorem.

Here are two microtheme assignments that Svitak assigns to her class in technical mathematics:

Congratulations! You just won the Superduper Lottery! You have a choice of Prize A or Prize B. Prize A is one million dollars a day for 30 days and you collect your total prize at the end of 30 days. Prize B starts out with two cents the first day, four cents the second day, eight cents the third day, 16 cents the fourth day, and so on for 30 days. At the end of 30 days you collect the sum total of the 30 days' earnings. Which prize would you choose and why?

Niagara Falls has frozen over and you want to see for yourself. You hop into your 450 mph jet with your best friend to fly directly to the Falls, which is about 450 miles and 10 degrees northwest of New York City. There is a 125 mph wind from the east. Explain to your friend that you are not really heading east to go west!

Another instructor, building on the success of assigning the micro-theme to his students in a class on electric-circuit analysis, decided to evaluate this assignment informally. He assigned three exams during the semester. One microtheme was assigned after the first exam, and two were assigned after the second to test the assumption that by increasing the amount of writing they were doing, students would be able to grapple successfully with the increasing complexity of the material. The micro-themes he assigned were a combination of the summary-writing micro-theme and the quandary-posing microtheme. Here is one example:

Dear Dr. Electron:

My professor is throwing circuit laws at us faster than Doc Gooden's fastball—Ohm's law, Kirchhoff's voltage law, Kirchhoff's current law, volt-age-divider rule, current-divider rule! Boy, with all these laws and rules no wonder you never see an electron in trouble with the law!

All kidding aside, Doc, please help me, and tell me in a clear way how to use each of these five laws and rules. This will mean a lot to me because my professor says that knowing them builds a strong foundation for tackling the fancy circuits in modern electronic devices.

Thanks a million, Doc!
Yours truly,
Izzy Smart

While this project did not meet many of the requirements of a formal evaluation, the instructor believes that microthemes can be used to improve students' grades, by helping them rewrite their notes in an organized fashion and use the microtheme as a study guide.

According to Svitak (personal communication, August 3, 1988) "Since using journal questions and microthemes, I find my students listen with greater attention, asking and responding more eagerly to questions in class. One of my students told me, 'Forcing myself to write about what I was doing in a precise linear way helped me to learn, understand, and remember both the mechanics and the underlying concepts of the material.' Writing-to-learn strategies mean active, self-reliant students. How can I not use them?"

Writing, these teachers agree, leads to action, and action leads to learning.

References

Ambron, J. "Writing to Improve Learning in Biology." *Journal of College Science Teaching*, 1987, *16* (4), 263–266.

Bean, J. C., Drenk, D., and Lee, F. D. "Microtheme Strategies for Developing Cognitive Skills." In C. W. Griffin (ed.), *Teaching Writing in All Disciplines*. New Directions for Teaching and Learning, no. 12. San Francisco: Jossey-Bass, 1982.

Papier, S. N. "Joining Freshman Orientation Concepts with Writing-Across-the-Curriculum." Unpublished manuscript, 1988.
Rennert, R. A. "Values Clarification, Journals and the Freshman Writing Course." In O. H. Clapp (ed.), *On Righting Writing.* Urbana, Ill.: National Council of Teachers of English, 1973.

Linda C. Stanley is professor of English and director of the English department writing program at Queensborough Community College, City University of New York. She is also director of the Queensborough Institute for Writing and Critical Thinking, which includes WAC programs at Queensborough and in the Borough of Queens high schools.

Influenced by WAC, faculty redesign traditional writing assignments not only to develop clarity and coherence in discipline-specific genres but also to promote learning.

Discipline-Specific Assignments: Primary Resources for Writing Across the Curriculum

Hannah Karp Laipson

While the major objective of WAC programs is to convince faculty across the disciplines to incorporate writing into their pedagogy, teachers in many subjects do assign writing. In most instances, however, these instructors have concentrated on what Britton and others (1975) call "transactional" writing—that is, writing intended for a reader, writing that, in the case of student writers, informs the reader of what the writer knows. Writing Across the Curriculum, by contrast, emphasizes language process or, as Fulwiler (1987, p. 4) states, "discovering, creating, and formulating ideas as well as communicating their substance to others."

Many community college faculty have not only incorporated generic writing (such as journals) into assignments but have also adapted the WAC approach to their own discipline-specific writing assignments, thus fulfilling the mandate that writing initiate students into the modes of discourse in their disciplines (see Chapter Four). These instructors have decided, for example, that while clarity and coherence are vital in every field of study, these features are especially important when fuzzy thinking may affect a patient's health, a business contract, or a mechanical system. The following writing strategies, including traditional discipline-specific genres like nursing charts and progress summaries and business case studies, merge rhetorical considerations with the writing-to-learn approach.

Hotel and Restaurant Management: Case Study

Dan Daly, coordinator of Quinsigamond Community College's program in hotel and restaurant management, stresses that increased writing provides

NEW DIRECTIONS FOR COMMUNITY COLLEGES, no. 73, Spring 1991 © Jossey-Bass Inc., Publishers

valuable benefits for student learning. He is convinced that writing assignments spark interest in the subject matter and supply added motivation.
He explains that writing forces logical thought, since putting words on
paper requires students to consider their views carefully. He assigns a case
study in the first few days of class that breaks the ice and leads to a
spirited discussion. As a result, he says, the likelihood of students' enthusiastic participation is greatly enhanced.

Daly believes that writing helps students clarify their thinking about management problems and discover sensible solutions to those problems. One
case study that he gives his classes is a letter of complaint addressed to a
major hotel chain from an irate parent whose son has had many frustrating
difficulties with the chain's LaGuardia Airport hotel, where he was stranded
because of flight delays. Daly instructs his students to carefully consider the
information in the letter and then address the following issues:

Problems and symptoms of problems

Reasons such problems arise, as well as any flaws in the front-office
systems

A "damage assessment" of how and to what degree the hotel chain
has been hurt

How the damage, if it is significant, can be minimized

How any damage could have been avoided in the first place, or if it
could not, why not

What action the students would take upon receiving such a letter.

Respiratory Therapy: Chart and Progress Summaries

Carol Erskine of the respiratory therapy program at Quinsigamond Community College illustrates her concern for clear formulation of ideas in the following instructions to students for completing chart and progress summaries:
"Chart summaries or progress notes convey essential information to the next
person taking care of a patient. Therefore, the information, although it must
be concise, must also be accurate and complete. Always remember that notes
in patients' charts are legally binding, so you can't say, 'I meant to say something else' or 'I just didn't write it the way it happened.'" Erskine laces her list
of rules for the assignment with points about the need for clear thinking and
communication. Students are told to write in complete sentences, for phrases
can be misinterpreted. Another rule is to convey all pertinent information in
an appropriate sequence: "You know what you did and what happened with
the patient, but that does not mean that anyone else will."

Nursing: Cultural Assessments and Their Implications
for Nursing Interventions

Frances Monahan, chair of nursing of Rockland Community College, shares
many concerns with Erskine. Monahan recognizes that the ability to write

clear, objective notes, patient-care summaries, and referrals to other health care professionals and community agencies is mandatory. The following assignment, by which students demonstrate their knowledge of cultural practices and the importance of such practices in planning and implementing nursing care, guides students by clearly indicating the requirements of content and form:

1. Select a cultural group of your choice (Native American, Chicano, Hasid, Haitian, African-American).
2. Describe the practices unique to that cultural group in relation to two of the following areas: food habits, hygiene, communication patterns, family life, and time orientation.
3. Discuss the implications of each area for the nursing care of an elderly member of that cultural group for whom you are caring in a chronic-illness setting. Assume that the patient in question is alert and not now considered terminal. Use specific examples of adjustments in nursing interventions.

Secretarial Studies: Case Studies

As Mary Belluardo tells her classes in secretarial studies at Quinsigamond Community College, anyone working in a modern office realizes the vast amount of paperwork created every day. It is produced not only by executives but also by their secretaries. Belluardo reminds her students that as secretaries or administrative assistants, they will need to go beyond the basic skills of grammar, punctuation, and spelling in their writing and be able to compose writing at their employers' request.

Belluardo also advises her students on the need for business correspondence to be clear, concise, natural, and friendly, which requires planning: messages should be adapted to their proper audiences. In urging them to get right to the point, without rambling on in excessive or redundant phrases, she tells them to emphasize the reader, not the writer: "No matter how angry someone makes you, never write in anger."

In the following two case studies, Belluardo engages her students in writing that requires sensitivity to audience, tone, and organization:

1. Your employer's friend has received a great honor. It was announced in the daily papers. Your employer asks you to compose a letter of congratulation for his signature. Make up an honor, names, and situation, and compose the letter. Let your imagination take off.
2. Try this: You work for Devine's Jewelers, a firm that sells glasses as well as jewelry. A customer ordered a set of wine glasses and a matching decanter. When the package arrived at the customer's residence, the contents were damaged. The customer has sent your company an irate letter, and you have been asked to respond. Write your response.

Accounting: Partnership Agreement

At Mesa Community College, John Mainieri approaches his accounting courses with pragmatic knowledge that he acquired in the business world. Why has he introduced writing into an accounting course?

"As an accountant progresses in an accounting firm," he says, "more and more time is spent communicating through the writing of memoranda, letters, footnotes to financial statements, and reports. Writing is no less important in the corporate accounting arena. Here, reports, proposals, and interpretations of financial data must also be written."

Mainieri assigns a partnership agreement because it governs how cash, income, and capital are distributed among partners. The culmination of students' work on partnerships is an individually prepared written agreement. Mainieri prepares his students for their writing assignments by giving them specific guidelines, so that their writing will reinforce their learning of the subject:

1. Decide on a name, location, and business purpose for your partnership.
2. Determine the duties of each of the partners and what he or she will contribute to the partnership as an initial investment.
3. Assume that the partnership had $100,000 of profit during the first year. How will you allocate the profit to the partners?
4. Determine how much of a draw each partner will be allowed.
5. What happens if another person wants to join the partnership?
6. What will happen if a partner wants to leave the partnership?
7. What will you do if all the partners agree that the partnership should be disbanded?
8. Suppose that one of your partners has spent all the partnership's cash, and then some. Assume that checks are bouncing all over town. What are the implications for the partnership and for each of the other partners?

Mainieri has found that small-group discussion of these questions in prewriting sessions help students considerably in preparing their individual agreements.

The several examples cited in this chapter illustrate that creative, discipline-centered writing assignments can be further strengthened by the adoption of WAC-oriented assignment designs. Some instructors have broken long assignments into parts, emphasizing process as well as product. Others have incorporated very specific instructions to guide their students through the process. Most have shown an awareness that establishment of audience and tone can produce effective results. In all the instances described here, language and thinking are inextricably bound.

When these instructors are asked what positive value they find in assigning writing to their students, they cite their students' increased ability to organize thoughts, explore options or solutions, and clarify fuzzy ideas, all of which increase the students' confidence in expressing themselves about the course content, in speaking as well as in writing.

References

Britton, J., Burgess, T., Martin, N., McLeod, A., and Rosen, H. *The Development of Writing Abilities.* New York: Macmillan, 1975.

Fulwiler, T. *Teaching with Writing.* Upper Montclair, N.J.: Boynton/Cook, 1987.

Hannah Karp Laipson is professor of English at Quinsigamond Community College, in Worcester, Massachusetts. She has been coordinator of the college's WAC program since it began in 1986.

*Three geographically diverse community colleges have implemented
writing-emphasis courses and demonstrated that WAC is no longer
merely a trend or an innovative idea but a real and necessary part
of every college curriculum.*

Formalizing WAC in the Curriculum: Writing-Emphasis Courses

*Patricia Durfee, Ann Sova, Libby Bay, Nancy Leech,
Robert Fearrien, Ruth Lucas*

After the workshops, and after the excitement of discovering that writing is
a unique tool for learning, faculty involved in WAC programs ask themselves, "How do we make writing a permanent feature of the academic
program?" In response to this need to incorporate writing permanently
into the curriculum, three community colleges have developed writing-
emphasis (or writing-intensive) courses. While precise motives and methods differ, each institution has drawn up plans for formulating and formal-
izing writing assignments in courses in each student's program of study.
While none of the three institutions has a program that is completely
formed, tested, and evaluated, their experiences may provide guidelines for
other community colleges at a similar juncture in their WAC programs.

Formulating the Writing-Emphasis Course: Broome Community College

In January 1989, students at Broome Community College (BCC) began
taking writing-emphasis ("W") courses in their degree programs. These
courses are the culmination of an eight-year collegial process: faculty discussions and debates, subcommittee study and recommendations, and,
finally, an affirmative, full-faculty vote on a general education curriculum
reform, of which the writing-emphasis courses are an integral part.

"W" courses at BCC are directly linked to a general education curricular reform that requires students who are receiving associate degrees to

take a first-semester writing-skills course taught by English faculty, followed by two writing-emphasis courses, at least one in a student's specialty. Finally, in the last semester, students enroll in an advanced, issues-oriented writing course taught by English faculty, which is intended to incorporate and synthesize core components of the general education curriculum.

"W" Course Guidelines. In 1986, BCC's WAC committee accepted the administrative task of establishing guidelines for the implementation of writing-emphasis courses. The committee's involvement was crucial, since the committee represented the entire campus academic population with its diversity of writing needs. Working from a consensus that students who write extensively in content courses will become more effective communicators, a WAC subcommittee, with members from the four college divisions, devised guidelines for the "W" courses. Briefly, the guidelines specify that students will produce 2,000 to 2,500 words of formal writing or writing intended for an audience. This formal writing should meet minimum standards of proficiency, which is defined rather traditionally as containing the following elements:

Clearly stated purpose (thesis or main idea)
Adequate support or development of the main idea
Clear and logical organization of information
Complete sentences
Standard usage of grammar, punctuation, and spelling
Correct documentation appropriate to the field.

Although outlined rather prescriptively in the guidelines, these standards are intended to be integrated by each professor according to the discipline and the nature of the assignment. The primary consideration in determining writing proficiency should be whether the paper communicates clearly and effectively in the context of the course.

The faculty who drew up the guidelines were sensitive to the fact that many teachers in disciplines other than English feel insecure about evaluating students' writing, either because of the time it requires or because they believe they lack the expertise. "W" course faculty are therefore encouraged not to accept papers that are poorly written, and to require students to seek help from the college's writing center in revising and resubmitting their work.

A significant feature of the guidelines is that they require the formal writing to display some evidence of critical thinking through thought-provoking, creative assignments based on the course objectives, rather than relying on conventional assignments, such as term papers and book reviews. Faculty are also encouraged to use a variety of informal, ungraded writing activities to stimulate greater student involvement and better learning. A major aspect of these guidelines is that they stimulate faculty to use writing as a problem-solving process.

Implementation. Since the WAC committee completed the guidelines before the faculty vote endorsing general education, the committee proposed a pilot program to test the effectiveness of "W" courses. The administration approved funding to train eight full-time faculty, two from each division, to plan and teach individual writing-emphasis courses according to the "W" course guidelines. Through a general campus announcement, faculty were invited to participate in a two-semester training program developed by English department consultants. In the fall of 1987, the selected faculty were paid a modest stipend to attend a one-day workshop immersing them in writing as a process. By writing and sharing, faculty explored their own experiences with writing, strategies for generating and developing ideas, types of problems encountered in using writing with students, and techniques for planning effective assignments. This session was essential: if faculty are ever to use writing successfully in the classroom, they must write themselves and reexperience the vulnerability of putting the self on paper. Two follow-up sessions were devoted to helping faculty plan assignments and write course outlines for the spring.

By the beginning of the spring 1988 semester, eight writing-emphasis courses were running at BCC. During this period, program participants were given release time equivalent to one course to attend a weekly seminar in which they shared experiences, read and discussed pertinent literature, and reacted to presentations by the seminar coordinators. These presentations focused on linking writing assignments to course objectives, planning effective assignments in content areas, understanding the composing process, evaluating students' writing, utilizing the writing center, and using writing to gain access to texts. By seminar's end, the interdisciplinary faculty had laid a realistic foundation for future "W" courses.

To prepare for full implementation of required "W" courses, the college offered another series of workshops in the fall of 1988. Since some "W" courses were to be multisection courses involving several instructors, some workshops were geared toward particular disciplines, while others were offered to the entire faculty. The coordinators also consulted with individual faculty about their specific writing concerns and began to construct a handbook for "W" course instructors.

An ongoing feature of this faculty development effort is the use of writing specialists to address faculty and conduct programs. Anticipating the move to "W" courses, the writing center is increasing its staff and will offer student workshops. In the future, the writing center will assume full responsibility for supporting "W" courses as WAC becomes a reality at Broome Community College.

Problems and Possible Solutions: Rockland Community College

Any WAC program that moves toward schoolwide writing courses invariably encounters difficulties. Problems at Rockland Community College have involved faculty and student reluctance, budget allocations, the inherent structure of a large project, and evaluation procedures. As a result, while Rockland has solved many of its problems, writing-emphasis courses on campus are still in their experimental stage.

Faculty's Reluctance. Engaging faculty (other than from the English department) in WAC is very difficult, chiefly because these faculty members believe writing to be the exclusive responsibility of the English department, and they do not want to devote classroom time to nondisciplinary content. They also do not feel confident about teaching writing. At Rockland, not all faculty are convinced that writing-emphasis courses will enhance their students' learning, but they have been persuaded that these courses need not involve actual writing instruction, since a writing-center referral system has been organized for referral of students who have severe writing problems.

Students' Hesitation. When students have the choice of enrolling either in writing-emphasis courses or traditional courses, most will avoid the writing-emphasis option. It is far better, during the initial and voluntary phases of introducing these courses, not to designate them in any way in course schedules, but rather simply to have instructors proceed with utilizing writing tasks as part of the curriculum. When "W" courses become a requirement, however, whether students hesitate or not, they have to register for them, just as they do for any other graduation requirement.

Inherent Structure. Two to three writing-emphasis courses are required of all students for graduation. When there is not enough faculty support for a requirement like Rockland's, a limited number of "W" courses in each discipline can be offered instead. If this limited experiment does not lead faculty to vote eventually for mandated "W" courses, the infusion model is another alternative: through a pilot project, consciousness can be so raised that instructors in all disciplines will be interested and willing to incorporate writing tasks into the curriculum, and students are then introduced to some writing in every course. A danger is that faculty will choose not to participate. At Rockland, however, a small but increasing number of instructors has become interested and involved. It is also essential, with this model, that the importance of writing be maintained in the public eye by a publication such as a writing-council newsletter, a magazine of students' work, a campus guide to writing tasks, or a college style sheet.

Evaluation. Evaluation has been the major problem in incorporating writing-emphasis courses at Rockland. In the first years of the WAC program, it was not clear whether the focus in "W" courses was writing to learn or learning to write. Therefore, although narrative evaluations by students and faculty were filled with praise and indications of achievement, the results of analytical evaluation of students' papers, which relied heavily on the improvement of surface writing features, were depressing. Since content-area teachers were not giving instruction in the mechanics of English, and since students did not utilize the writing center, more could not have been expected. One important lesson has been that formal evaluation should be avoided, if at all possible, until the program has been tested, revised, and retested. Nevertheless, some credence should be given to impressionistic narrative evaluations, as well as to statistical tabulations, because teachers and students alike know when learning is occurring. Having solved many problems, Rockland is optimistic about the future of writing-emphasis courses at the institution.

Elements Required for Approval and Success: Kapiolani Community College

The experience of Kapiolani Community College suggests that a faculty-engendered and -sponsored effort provides a solid basis for creating a WAC program. When faculty are convinced of the value of WAC, they will participate in workshops and put in additional hours to revise syllabi and make writing a necessary, vital part of the learning program. Specifically because of enthusiasm for the informal approach, Kapiolani was not optimistic about institutionalizing courses with a writing emphasis. Nevertheless, faculty have come to see their value, and what we wish to discuss here is how such courses' success has been guaranteed.

Sowing the Seeds. From its beginning almost a decade ago, the WAC movement has spread on the Kapiolani campus and now includes more than eighty instructors who assign writing in liberal arts as well as vocational programs. After the WAC project had been operating for half a dozen years, Kapiolani's senior institution, the University of Hawaii at Manoa, which draws most of the school's transfer students, mandated a phased-in requirement for writing-emphasis or writing-intensive courses to be completed by students seeking bachelor's degrees. The university probably took this route because it is more difficult for a four-year institution to launch an informal WAC project such as Kapiolani's, but the informal approach has the potential for involving more faculty, particularly those who like to meet in workshops with other faculty, an activity that this mandate sidesteps.

Bringing in the Sheaves. Despite our reservations about formally mandated writing-intensive courses in response to the writing-intensive requirement, Kapiolani is moving to introduce W-I courses. The Manoa campus has stipulated that instructors will interact with students in the writing process in classes of no more than twenty students. Another essential guideline is that writing is to grow out of subject matter, reinforcing the current belief that writing helps a student discover what he or she knows about a subject. At least sixteen pages, or four thousand words, are required of each student in a semester's time, and this writing represents a major part of the student's grade. Eventually, five such courses will be required for a degree—three in the lower division and two in the upper.

At our campus, after considerable debate in the academic-standards committee, the curriculum committee, and the faculty senate, additional standards have been established. First, a freshman expository-writing course will be a prerequisite for enrollment in a W-I course. Second, most of the writing will be informal, rather than formal. While some scholars contend that learning logs and journals dilute the intellectual process, those involved at Kapiolani believe that these forms of writing help students understand the subject. Third, one-quarter of the semester's grade will be based on students' ability to express themselves about course content through writing. Finally, 50 percent of writing assignments must be completed satisfactorily for a student to earn a grade of C or better in a course.

The process of approving writing-intensive courses on the Kapiolani campus was often painful, involving questions of quality, amount of writing required, academic freedom, hiring policies, and alternative forms of learning. One point that was insisted on throughout was that participation by faculty should continue to be voluntary. Spirited discussion on these matters was vital to ensuring total campus support for the W-I proposal.

On the basis of Kapiolani's experience with implementation writing-intensive courses, the following recommendations are offered:

1. Keep faculty informed of what you are doing and plan to do, through campus publications, memos, hearings, and departmental meetings, so that everyone understands what is expected and what is on the agenda of campus committees concerned with the curriculum.
2. Form a writing committee or task force to advise the coordinators and to serve as advocates for what is being proposed.
3. Do not expect to get universal approval of what you are doing. Pockets of resistance will help you focus on potential problems. Expect that some faculty will have little interest in WAC.
4. Always keep in mind that you want to benefit the students. You can frequently sell a proposal that is difficult for administrators and faculty to accept by emphasizing how much students will benefit from it.
5. Be sure to give faculty an opportunity to acquire effective techniques for working with students through their writing processes.

The Harvest. Kapiolani introduced its writing-intensive courses in the spring of 1989. It was expected that most faculty volunteers would come from the social sciences and humanities, and this is what happened. Some transfer-level vocational courses have also been included, however. The process for the introduction of writing-intensive courses is to have faculty write applications for their classes to be designated as W-I courses, with an outline of the instructional procedures to support such designation. These applications are examined by the WAC coordinators and by a writing committee. Initially, all applications were accepted, with encouragement and additional assistance furnished by the coordinators for those instructors whose applications suggested that their authors needed more help. By an agreement with the curriculum committee, a list of courses accepted for the W-I designation is furnished to committee members and the faculty senate. Students are informed through catalogue and course schedule statements and through articles in the campus newspaper about the W-I policy.

Of course, not all community colleges are subject to mandates by larger university systems, although this may increasingly become the case. Whatever the initial reason for instituting writing-intensive courses, they are expected to be a vital part of the larger WAC emphasis at Kapiolani.

Conclusion

From institution to institution, the immediate reasons vary for seeking writing-emphasis mandates, as do the problems encountered in the process and the specific requirements of the writing-emphasis courses themselves. None of the three institutions discussed in this chapter has a program of writing-emphasis courses that is completely formed, tested, and evaluated, for the concept is too new. All three programs, however, demonstrate that WAC is no longer merely a trendy or innovative idea but is on its way to becoming a real and necessary part of every college tradition.

Patricia Durfee and Ann Sova have been coordinating the WAC program at Broome Community College, including the development of writing-emphasis courses, for the past four years.

Libby Bay is professor of English and department chair at Rockland Community College.

Nancy Leech is director of the writing center at Rockland Community College and head of the writing-intensive program there.

Robert Fearrien, a history instructor, was a coordinator of WAC at Kapiolani Community College until December 1988.

Until her recent retirement, Ruth Lucas was a WAC coordinator and an English instructor at Kapiolani Community College.

A WAC evaluation project is multifaceted, participative, and formative and requires close coordination with the WAC program itself for effective implementation.

Organizing a WAC Evaluation Project: Implications for Program Planning

Gail Hughes-Wiener, Susan K. Jensen-Cekalla

The Minnesota Community College System comprises eighteen colleges, ranging in size from a few hundred students to over six thousand. These colleges, operating semiautonomously but within centrally administered guidelines, are scattered throughout the state—in urban, suburban, agricultural, mining, and forested settings. Nearly two thousand faculty deal firsthand with widely diverse students, an increasingly large proportion of whom are returning, nontraditional students with jobs and families.

An extensive WAC program has been operating in the Minnesota Community College System since 1985. The program, funded by the Bush Foundation and recently renewed for three years, is built around an annual summer conference that brings together faculty from all eighteen colleges in the system, an annual reunion conference, and a multifaceted follow-up support system that continues during the academic year at the individual colleges. Follow-up support includes tutoring, materials and supplies, informal meetings, in-house and outside consulting, and modest release time for a WAC coordinator at each college to lead the local program. A full-time faculty WAC coordinator for the whole system works with the system's director of staff development and the college faculty WAC coordinators to define the goals and direction of the program.

Throughout its life, the WAC program has been accompanied by an ambitious evaluation project, also funded by the Bush Foundation. The program's evaluation coordinator, who spends half her time on the WAC evaluation project, is responsible for its design and administration, and a part-time statistician is responsible for computerized analysis of quantitative data. External consultants knowledgeable about the assessment of students' writing and educational measurement assist the project.

The major goal of the evaluation project is to determine whether the WAC program helps students improve their writing ability and subject-specific learning. To interpret the results, it is also necessary to identify the extent to which the program has affected the use of writing activities in the classroom, for if there has not been a change in instruction, an increase in students' learning cannot be attributed to the WAC program. In addition, the project collects information about participants' reactions to the WAC program, for use by program coordinators in the planning of future activities. Implementing this broad-based evaluation requires the assistance of WAC program coordinators and the active, ongoing participation of large numbers of faculty.

Components of the WAC Evaluation Project

The evaluation project casts a wide net to describe a variety of effects from the WAC program. To obtain needed information, surveys were completed by faculty and students. Faculty were interviewed, students' essays were collected, and instructional experiments were conducted in biology, business, philosophy, and English classes. Each of these information-gathering tasks represents one component of the evaluation project, which required its own planning, organization, and coordination with the WAC program.

Workshop Surveys. Faculty who attended the four-day WAC summer workshop completed several different types of surveys to obtain feedback about the workshop's content and organization. Upon arrival, they answered a fifteen-item questionnaire on their assumptions about the use of instructional writing, which was related to key objectives of the WAC program. The results were tabulated on the spot and given to the workshop facilitator, so that he would know what to emphasize in his presentations. Participants completed the questionnaire again at the conclusion of the workshop. The pre- and postworkshop results gave the program organizers an indication of how effective the workshop was in communicating the content of the WAC program. Participants were also asked to complete a conventional workshop-evaluation form, which asked for their reactions to each of the workshop sessions. A short survey was also designed to pinpoint topics and concerns that college WAC coordinators could pursue at follow-up meetings during the year. Several weeks after the workshop, participants were sent a short-answer questionnaire, which asked for their reactions to the workshop after they had had a chance to reflect on their experience.

Faculty and Student Surveys. At the end of one academic year, and again at the end of the three-year project, WAC faculty participants completed a survey, which asked for their perceptions of the program's effects on themselves and their students. These surveys were given to obtain feedback after participants had had time to experiment with the use of writing activities in their classes and to see whether participants had continued to use writing activities over the course of the program. Students were given a parallel survey, so that the perceptions of students and faculty could be compared.

Faculty Interviews. Hour-long interviews were given to a random sample of forty WAC participants, stratified to ensure representation of faculty at a variety of colleges and in a variety of subject areas. The interviews provided in-depth information about the use of writing activities and about faculty's perceptions of their effectiveness. They also enabled the evaluation project to check the validity of answers obtained on faculty surveys, which asked some of the same questions in less detail.

Students' Compositions. Seventeen volunteer faculty—most but not all of them WAC participants—were recruited to serve as raters of students' compositions. At an initial workshop, participants were trained to use a holistic evaluation method, and they prepared several essay questions to be pilot-tested. After the essays were collected from students in a number of classes, a second workshop was held to score the compositions for quality of writing and to select and revise the essay question that had proved most effective for this purpose. A preliminary scoring guide was also constructed. After a second test of the revised question, approximately 1,200 essays were collected. The compositions were rated, without the raters' knowledge of who had written them, at a final two-day rating workshop. Each student submitting an essay was given a "WAC'iness" score based on the number of classes he or she completed with WAC-trained instructors, plus composition courses. Results were analyzed to see whether students who had more experience with instructional writing (as reflected by the "WAC'iness" score) received higher ratings on their essays.

Subject Experiments. Faculty in subject areas that had the largest number of WAC participants—biology, business, social science, and English—were recruited to conduct experiments in which instructional writing was used with some students but not with others. Approximately half a dozen faculty in each of these subjects attended a training workshop, at which some participants designed an experiment suitable for their situations and all received training as trait raters (trait rating is an adaptation of holistic rating, which, in our project, focused on subject objectives identified by participating experimenters). Most of the experiments involved two sections of the same class, both taught by the experimenter. An essay exam, a business letter, or some other exam involving subjective judgment was collected from students in both sections and was rated by faculty in the subject group at a final rating workshop. Results were analyzed to see whether the students who had received instructional writing achieved higher ratings on their essay exams than students who had received another type of instruction.

Coordination Between the WAC Program and the Evaluation Project

Our WAC evaluation is highly participative in its design. The interview script, essay question and scoring guide, and subject experiments were developed, pilot-tested, revised, administered, and scored by faculty who were trained to implement these components of the project. The evaluation coordinator worked closely with the system's WAC coordinator in constructing faculty and student surveys to ensure that they were relevant to program needs and interests. All participants were asked to complete several faculty surveys. In addition, thirty-four instructors collected students' essays and forty others collected surveys of students in one or more classes.

In a project of this nature, the evaluation coordinator becomes just that—someone who coordinates activities with the WAC program to ensure that the components of the evaluation project are effectively organized and implemented. WAC program personnel make critical contributions to the evaluation project through their collaboration with evaluation personnel in creating a positive attitude toward evaluation, organizing data flow, developing instruments, and using the information collected.

Creating a Positive Attitude Toward Evaluation. Before recruiting faculty to fill out surveys, undertake training, and design experiments for their classes, we had to create a positive attitude toward the very notion of evaluation. We recognized that the idea of evaluation can generate apprehension and skepticism—apprehension that results may be used to discredit the WAC program, which has enjoyed strong faculty support, and skepticism that any useful, valid results could be found. WAC coordinators made special efforts to explain to their colleagues that the latter group's participation was a way to contribute to the strengthening of the WAC program and was an opportunity for personal and professional growth.

Organizing Data Flow. Conducting any large-scale, systemwide project requires considerable effort to communicate necessary information. Information about evaluation activities is disseminated through the WAC workshop, WAC mailings and newsletters, and WAC coordinators at their colleges, as well as by phone and mail from the program evaluator. Attendance by the evaluation coordinator at the summer workshop and other WAC activities assists communication and helps build trust in the evaluation project.

Developing Instruments and Experiments. It has been essential for the program evaluator to understand the basic assumptions of our WAC program. As the program has matured, we have been moving from an emphasis on writing to an emphasis on thinking. During the three final years of the six-year grant, our summer conference will focus on how the Perry Model of Intellectual Development in College can help teachers understand the dynamics of their classrooms and shape a total teaching strategy, including writing activities, that stimulates students' intellectual development. Through her participation in WAC program activities and through our physical proximity (we share an office), the program evaluator has a clear understanding of what we are trying to do and of how our focus on the total classroom has intensified. Because of her intimate acquaintance with our goals and direction, she has been able to tailor survey questions and experiments to reflect our evolving concerns.

Using the Information. WAC coordinators attempt to make good use of the information and opportunities that the evaluation project provides. The program evaluator quantifies, summarizes, and reproduces the results of questionnaires and surveys, which provide information that we integrate into the shaping of future summer conferences and follow-up activities. We have also been able to apply our newly developed skills in holistic rating and trait rating to the WAC program. One of the perennial concerns of faculty is how to respond to students' writing fairly and efficiently. Our training in holistic scoring has helped us deal with this issue. Because of the WAC program's collaboration with the evaluation project, we have a team trained and ready to share what we know with the rest of the faculty in the system.

Results of the Evaluation Project

What has the evaluation project been able to demonstrate about our WAC program to date? Workshop surveys show that WAC participants are enthusiastic about the program. End-of-year surveys and faculty interviews indicate that participants are using more types of instructional writing and perceive their use of writing activities to be more effective than it was before they entered the program. Attendance data show that the program is filled to capacity each year and that participants come from a broad range of colleges and subject areas. In other words, we have considerable evidence that the program is well administered and that it is affecting the instructional methods used by WAC faculty in their own classrooms.

Has this increase in writing shown any benefits for students? Results from the composition study show that students who had more experience with instructional writing did receive higher scores on their essays than the other students. The difference in scores was small but statistically significant. Moreover, students who were in a political science class designed specifically according to WAC principles received the highest mean of the forty-eight classes involved in the study. More research is needed to determine whether these positive outcomes can be attributed to the use of writing apart from other possible factors. The results to date, however, provide convincing evidence that if activities are well designed and well implemented, instructional writing can help students become better writers. This should alleviate concerns (see Chapter Four) that the informal, private writing so pervasive in WAC programs may not contribute to the development of formal writing skills.

Results from the subject experiments were promising but inconclusive. In five of the six studies, students in the class section that used instructional writing obtained slightly higher mean scores on their essay exams than did students in the section that used some other method. These differences were not statistically significant, however, and thus may have been due to chance. As has been seen in efforts to improve the quality of students' compositions, it may be that the use of instructional writing per se may not be of much benefit but that well-designed assignments that enable students to translate the formal discourse of a field into their own personal meanings will enhance students' understanding of course material. For example, reflective writing (see Chapter Three) may be more effective than assignments that ask for simple recall. Further experiments are needed to test the effects of different types of writing assignments and assignment designs.

Survey responses indicate that students and faculty alike favor the use of instructional writing. Students who reported having had more experience with instructional writing also had more positive attitudes toward writing, but even those who reported little experience were positive.

In addition to obtaining encouraging results, the evaluation project has become a valuable adjunct to the WAC program itself. The information gathered will help us refine the WAC program, the use of instructional writing, and the methods used to assess students' writing. Faculty who participated in the evaluation activities have acquired new skills as interviewers, holistic raters, and essay raters, as well as greater understanding and appreciation of program evaluation and instructional research.

Gail Hughes-Wiener is coordinator of program evaluation and instructional research for WAC and other programs funded by the Bush Foundation in the Minnesota Community College System.

Susan K. Jensen-Cekalla, a faculty member at Inver Hills Community College, serves as statewide coordinator of the WAC program in the Minnesota Community College System.

The WAC programs at three colleges illustrate the different shapes that diverse linguistic environments may impose on efforts to foster Writing Across the Curriculum in community colleges.

Adapting Language Across the Curriculum to Diverse Linguistic Populations

Linda Hirsch, Joanne Nadal, Linda Shohet

In the past decade, programs that emphasize Language Across the Curriculum, or the use of talk and writing as learning tools, have been proliferating on college campuses, not only because educators are coming to understand the connection between language and learning but also because the model is flexible enough to be adapted to diverse socioeconomic and political contexts. The three colleges discussed in this chapter illustrate how programs responding to similar problems have taken different shapes, according to their diverse linguistic environments.

Addressing the Needs of ESL Students: A Tutorial Model

Background. If America's native speakers of English are in the throes of a literacy crisis, then the linguistic problems of second-language learners, who continue to enter our schools in growing numbers, are even greater. They are frequently unable to compete successfully in academic courses and, without programs to address their needs, may be considered disenfranchised. Hostos Community College of the City University of New York, an open-admissions, urban bilingual college with an incoming freshman class that is 89 percent Spanish-speaking, is committed to meeting the needs of its predominantly ESL population.

ESL students' poorly developed language skills, combined with traditional lecture- and textbook-mode pedagogies, often result in their not sufficiently understanding course material. Foremost among their problems is their inability to synthesize and paraphrase information quickly enough to take notes from lectures or textbooks. They also have difficulty understanding discipline-specific vocabulary. Their academic performance is further hindered by the high reading level of most textbooks, by their limited English-language oral proficiency, which inhibits their classroom participation, and by writing tasks whose complexities surpass their emerging skills.

Rationale. To address the needs of these students and improve their retention, Hostos Community College has developed a tutoring model that draws on several principles developed by the Language Across the Curriculum movement. The project's approach is to use "expressive function" talk and writing (Britton and others, 1975). This function is described as the language closest to natural speech and focuses on fluency, rather than on explicitness or correctness. It is ideally suited to the exploration of ideas and is often the language of the first draft. In addition, the project draws on research that suggests that learning is an active, ongoing process in which the mind makes meaning from experience (Berthoff, 1981; Britton, 1970; Kelly, 1963). Thus, the project stresses that language—both talking and writing—plays an important role in the learning process.

Program Description. The project places upper-level ESL students, together with those who have completed an ESL sequence of study but lack the writing skills required for admission to freshman composition, into tutor-led groups linked to particular courses. Each group of four to seven students meets for an hour and a half once a week during the fourteen-week academic semester. The learning strategy is expressive talk and writing in a pupil-centered learning environment. Tutors play a less than usually dominant role and give students more responsibility for their own learning. During group sessions, students first paraphrase course material in their own words. Then, through talk and writing, they establish points of connection between new and known material, a process essential for true learning. Students thus lessen their dependency on tutors and teachers by learning from each other. Writing is used both as a means of discovery and as a way of synthesizing and recording material.

The tutorial group process was selected because it incorporates many of the principles of a language-for-learning model. For example, its small size and informality readily elicit the oral discourse vital to the development of writing and to the corresponding comprehension of course material. Furthermore, the tutor is not an authority figure or evaluator of students' performance. The tutor's stance as a fellow inquirer frees ESL students to participate more actively in the learning process.

Extensive tutor training is an essential component of this model. Tutors meet as a group, led by the project director, for two weeks before their group assignments. Their training enables them to experience the very process through which they will be guiding students. They continue to meet once a week for an hour and a half throughout the semester. In addition to acquainting them with relevant research and tutoring techniques, training sessions give tutors the opportunity to share problems and successes and obtain ongoing feedback and support. Once a week, tutors are required to attend the content class that group members are taking and to submit detailed reports of each group session.

Conclusions. Since its inception in 1982, this model has been rigorously evaluated through both quantitative and qualitative means (Hirsch, 1986, 1988). In comparing teacher-assigned final grades of project participants to grades of nonparticipants in the same class, the results are seen to be significant at the .05 level. Project participation has proved a discernible factor in students' improved academic performance and retention.

Preparing Bilingual Students for Transfer

Background. Miami–Dade Community College has reaffirmed its commitment to the transfer mission of the community college and to a curriculum that serves as a conduit for academic success in senior institutions. Germane to this commitment is the retention and instruction of nontraditional students, many of whom are former ESL graduates. Notwithstanding the many nonacademic factors that influence students' performance and continuance in college, Miami–Dade supports the idea that transfer should remain a viable option and is taking aggressive steps to ensure retention. Among these steps is a new appraisal of Writing Across the Curriculum as an innovative curricular model for the cognitive and linguistic needs of bilingual students.

Rationale. ESL students have often been considered high-risk college enrollees by virtue of their limited practice in reading and writing English. The research of Ramirez (1973) and Anderson (1988) indicates cognitive factors, independent of practice, that express students' knowledge or understanding of an assignment. Anderson suggests that many nontraditional students have learned to communicate in a mode different from that of the Western European tradition. He calls this mode *field-dependence* and says that it is reflected in a communication style characterized as subjective, affective, and imagerial. By contrast, Western thinking, or *field-independence*, emphasizes written expression that is formal, objective, impersonal, and empirical. Educators who are unaware of culturally based differences in communication and in thinking/learning styles may be misassessing nontraditional students' academic progress.

The InterAmerican Center of the Wolfson Campus of Miami–Dade and its English communications department have therefore opted to introduce WAC early in the academic career of nontraditional students. The center's personnel believe that WAC can and should cultivate a literacy level conducive to transfer, one that will initiate students into the rhetorical modes and philosophical bases of specific discourse communities and help them compensate for what some claim to be the lowered literacy standards of open-access institutions. InterAmerican's program begins by isolating and reinforcing the linguistic skills that are prerequisites for academic writing. The program then exposes students to the specific rhetorical modes of the humanities and the social and natural sciences. Simultaneously, it seeks to raise basic literacy through reading, writing assignments, and individualized prescriptions for remedial work to be done independently by students in the center's computer laboratory.

Program Description. The initial classroom phase of the WAC program encompasses a series of readings designed to identify and afford practice in linguistic structures common to the Western communication style, such as indefinite pronouns, the passive voice, the use of the present and present-perfect tenses, and conjunctive adverbs. Students are then given writing exercises, such as simple summaries of reading selections, with which to practice these structures. Since summaries and critiques constitute many college and professional writing assignments, students are given ample opportunity to practice these developmental patterns in response to generic readings. After approximately twelve course hours, students begin to focus on discipline-specific reading and writing activities.

Reading and writing activities in the second phase of InterAmerican's WAC program address the conceptual frameworks and stylistic diversity of the humanities and the social and natural sciences. In-class readings emphasize the persuasive writing found in primary sources, instead of the expository writing in secondary sources, the English communications department also collaborates actively with disciplinary faculty in selecting readings and designing complementary writing assignments. This bilateral effort is greatly enhanced by collateral readers, selected part-time faculty who analyze, for structure and organization, students' essays that are submitted to them by WAC faculty. WAC faculty are free to analyze essays for content rather than style and to incorporate more meaningful and frequent writing assignments into their respective courses. Finally, all students in the WAC program are given individual prescriptions in the computer laboratory. These assignments are monitored and evaluated throughout the semester by laboratory and WAC staff. The assignments include a wide variety of reading and writing practice, remediation, and reinforcement of field-independent structures.

Conclusions. Many factors affect retention and transfer of nontraditional students. WAC as a particular retention strategy is currently being tested empirically at the Wolfson Campus and its InterAmerican Center. The college expects research to show how significantly WAC can improve the cognitive and linguistic skills of students and provide an academic initiative for students who might otherwise become a silent majority on urban campuses.

English as a Minority Language

Language is much debated in Canada, a bilingual country where English and French are constitutionally enshrined as the two official languages. About 75 percent of the Canadian population speaks and uses English except in the province of Quebec, where 80 percent of the population is French-speaking. A resurgence of French nationalism in Quebec in the 1960s led to the election in 1975 of a separatist government, which passed Bill 101, declaring Quebec unilingually French. Among many provisions, it restricted parents' choice of the language of schooling for their children. Unless both parents can prove that they were educated in English, they must register their children in French schools until the end of high school. Most immigrants are not entitled to English education, and Quebec remains the one place in North America where English is officially a minority language.

In Quebec, language is politics, and people are passionate about protecting and enhancing their mother tongue. Everyone is identified by mother tongue as francophone, anglophone, or allophone (having a mother tongue other than French or English). This preoccupation with language makes Montreal a culturally rich city but one always conscious of linguistic tension. The school system is a microcosm of language sensitivities. Only at the college level do the language restrictions on education drop, bringing into the English-speaking colleges many students with little or inadequate previous experience with English.

Background. Dawson College is the largest in Quebec's system of colleges, or *collèges de l'enseignement géneralé et professionel* (CEGEPs), with a full-time day enrollment of about 6,500. As one of the four English-speaking CEGEPs, Dawson encounters many students with language problems, including large numbers of ESL students, as well as underprepared native speakers and linguistically confused allophones.

In 1984, to address teachers' increasing complaints about literacy and resources, the Dawson academic senate established a two-year pilot project to complement special programs and support services but focus on changing teaching practices in all disciplines and integrating all the modes of language use. Because the word *language* is so charged in Quebec, Dawson chose to call the project Literacy Across the Curriculum. To emphasize that its audience is teachers, the program is housed in the faculty development department. Both choices have shaped the project.

Rationale. The model was drawn from the work of Britton and his colleagues (1970, 1975) and others on language, thought, and learning. Britton's work reveals that teaching practices and school policies are not informed by an understanding of the connection between language and learning and have rarely allowed students to use their own language to make sense of new material. He and others stress that teachers must give students the opportunity to use personal language to internalize new knowledge. They also remind teachers that research cannot be translated into teaching kits without allowance for the same process of development that we demand for our students (Britton, 1982). In this context, teachers become students and cannot be expected to change their practices in the absence of understanding.

Program Description. The program structure reflects the commitment to change among teachers. In regular workshops and collaborative group meetings, participating teachers voluntarily learn how to build talking, read-' ing, and writing into coursework in all disciplines. They share their frustrations and their triumphs, drawing strength from the support group, which also serves as a model of positive classroom organization, incorporating talk, drafting, peers' responses, and formal presentations.

The second premise of the project is that literacy must be addressed in its broadest context. The rationale is that recent insights into basic literacy can guide effective teaching practices inside institutions as well as outside (Freire, 1970, 1985; Shor, 1987). These insights suggest that literacy cannot be divorced from culture and personal motivation, that students must have some stake in defining learning objectives, and that learning need not be confined to classrooms. By focusing on literacy rather than on writing alone, Dawson has been able to present the issue of advanced literacy in the schools as part of a continuum. The college has forged links with adult and community literacy groups, created a resource center for information and materials on all aspects of literacy, and sponsored forums and conferences for tutors, teachers, and researchers. Five times per year, the project publishes the widely disseminated *Literacy Across the Curriculum,* a bulletin with research reports, reviews, and ideas for teaching language and learning.

As the first Canadian college to develop and maintain a fully funded project in this area, Dawson has become a center of interest. Many French educators who traditionally have had minimal connection with the English sector have begun to affiliate themselves with it, recognizing that a common concern for enhancing mother-tongue literacy, regardless of language, may be a bond rather than a barrier. Dawson's experience reveals that Language Across the Curriculum is an educational reform movement driven as much by politics as by theory.

Conclusion

In an effort to improve the learning of students in diverse linguistic environments, each of these three programs has chosen a different emphasis. Hostos Community College emphasizes the role that tutors can play in improving students' learning through writing and speaking. The Wolfson campus of Miami-Dade Community College stresses the literacy skills needed in the disciplines to enable bilingual students to transfer successfully to four-year programs. Dawson College has fused faculty workshops with extensive promotion of the value of talk and writing throughout the linguistically sensitive province of Quebec. What the programs have in common is their emphasis on the value of talk and writing for students' learning.

References

Anderson, J. A. "Cognitive Styles and Multicultural Populations." *Journal of Teacher Education*, 1988, *39* (1), 2-8.

Berthoff, A. E. *The Making of Meaning*. Upper Montclair, N.J.: Boynton/Cook, 1981.

Britton, J. *Language and Learning*. Harmondsworth, England: Penguin Books, 1970.

Britton, J. *Prospect and Retrospect: Selected Essays*. Upper Montclair, N.J.: Boynton/Cook, 1982.

Britton, J., Burgess, T., Martin, N., McLeod, A., and Rosen, H. *The Development of Writing Abilities*. London: Macmillan, 1975.

Freire, P. *Pedagogy of the Oppressed*. New York: Continuum, 1970.

Freire, P. *The Politics of Education*. South Hadley, Mass.: Bergin & Garvey, 1985.

Hirsch, L. "The Use of Expressive-Function Talk and Writing as a Learning Tool with Adult ESL Students Across the Curriculum." Unpublished doctoral dissertation, New York University, 1986.

Hirsch, L. "Language Across the Curriculum: A Model for ESL Students in Content Courses." In S. Benesch (ed.), *Ending Remediation: Linking ESL and Content in Higher Education*. Washington, D.C.: TESOL, 1988.

Kelly, G. A. *A Theory of Personality*. New York: Norton, 1963.

Ramirez, M. "Cognitive Styles and Cultural Democracy in Education." *Social Science Quarterly*, 1973, *53*, 895-904.

Shor, I. (ed.). *Freire for the Classroom: A Sourcebook for Liberatory Teaching*. Portsmouth, N.H.: Heinmann Educational Books, 1987.

Linda Hirsch is an assistant professor at Hostos Community College, where she teaches ESL, writing, and reading. She is content-tutor coordinator and directs the tutorial program described in this chapter.

Joanne Nadal teaches in the English department of the InterAmerican Center of the Wolfson Campus of Miami–Dade Community College. She has coordinated its WAC program since 1986.

Linda Shohet teaches English at Dawson College, Montreal, where she coordinates Literacy Across the Curriculum.

Integrated skills reinforcement (ISR) is a faculty development program that trains subject-area teachers in strategies that help students use all their language skills—reading, writing, speaking, and listening—to learn course content.

Literacy and Learning: Integrated Skills Reinforcement

JoAnn Romeo Anderson, Nora Eisenberg, Harvey S. Wiener

Over the past two decades, students with steadily declining abilities have come to college in increasing numbers. Many students with serious weaknesses in basic skills have been sitting in both college and high school classrooms, and many faculty seeing such students and such skills have been teaching courses that often bypass analytical approaches to content through reading, writing, and speaking. The crisis in literacy has become a crisis in learning, for the two are inextricably connected: language is the means to content, and content provides the necessary context for developing and advancing linguistic and analytical abilities. Basic-skills programs—remedial programs, if you will—cannot alone prepare students adequately for the demands of the various disciplines. Therefore, the responsibility for overseeing not just the learning of content but also literacy in relation to content has passed on to the subject-area teacher.

Yet, while more and more teachers recognize this responsibility, they also sense their lack of preparation to meet it. Graduate schools prepare college teachers in their fields of inquiry, but these teachers often have to pick up pedagogy on the job. Even high school teachers, although trained in methods, generally are not trained in methods that address literacy and learning for a growing segment of today's students.

In 1978, LaGuardia Community College, a branch of the City University of New York (CUNY), set out to develop a program to redress the problem of literacy and learning, a program that would draw dedicated teachers into the search for solutions. Not surprisingly, the task was complicated. The literature tended to focus on the reasons why language skills should be reinforced in content classes, not on specific techniques to help students make better use of their linguistic skills in exploring the disciplines. Further, what little had been done in this area in the United States generally focused on only one skills area, most often writing but, occasionally, reading. No programs at that time focused on integrating reading, writing, oral, and aural skills, yet an integrated program seemed essential. In Britain, for example, a governmental committee set up to address and redress declining reading skills asserted that expressive (speaking, writing) and receptive (listening, reading) modes of language were crucially interwoven. When the committee made its final recommendations, it called not for a national policy on reading but for a policy of Language Across the Curriculum. Our program honored this recommendation.

Finding no linguistically integrated model to draw on, we turned to our own experiences. We began with the premise that good teachers, as they work with students, almost instinctively discover strategies for strengthening students' use of language in learning course content. These strategies anchor the teaching of content. Perhaps, for example, a teacher begins the course by previewing with students the overall structure of the text. She points out that subheadings provide a running outline of the content covered and thus help students develop a mental schema for the material ahead. Perhaps a teacher gives students sets of thought-provoking questions to guide reading or focus listening in a lecture or discussion, or she provides students with repeated opportunities to use writing in summarizing knowledge, reinforcing procedures, analyzing arguments, or even identifying areas of confusion. Whatever strategy any one teacher creates, chances are that some colleague in another area or even at another institution has already discovered it or may discover it soon.

Such reinvention of the wheel seemed to us a waste of valuable time. Therefore, during the 1978–79 academic year, at the behest of and with support from LaGuardia's dean of faculty, Martin Moed, and with the collaboration of our colleagues, especially Carol Rivera-Kron and John Holland, we drew together successful language-rich approaches to curriculum from teachers in liberal arts, science, and professional areas. In the following academic year, we piloted these strategies with teachers across subject areas to determine which strategies would be most widely effective. The most successful approaches were collected in a text that became the cornerstone of a faculty development program rooted in concern for student learning. The most significant feature of this text, we believe, is that good teachers "find themselves" in various parts of it. As they leaf through the text, faculty in the program can often be heard to say, "I do this." What they also say is that they like the way the strategies are presented, in step-by-step fashion, allowing faculty to incorporate and adapt them easily. With its five major divisions (assessing students' communication skills in relation to content courses, helping students write for content courses, encouraging students' effective use of oral and listening skills in content courses, helping students read in content courses, and integrating language skills for content mastery), the text allows teachers to build courses on a firm foundation of literacy. We call our overall approach *integrated skills reinforcement* (ISR).

A Student-Centered Approach to Faculty Development

The ISR text was an important development, providing faculty with practical advice for bringing language strategies (reading, writing, speaking, and listening) to bear on particular course content. At the time we wrote the book, however, it was clear that our faculty wanted more than a reference manual. They wanted a program that would help them facilitate real change in their classrooms, and so we set out to develop such a program, paying close attention to the factors now seen as essential to success in training. First, we committed the program to the principles of collaboration and collegiality. Instructional development programs too often fail because they approach the teacher as the problem instead of recognizing the teacher as the agent for change. At LaGuardia, we began with the assumption that our teachers had enormous talent as classroom instructors. We asked our teachers to reflect on their experiences and to address these questions: What problems are students experiencing in dealing effectively with coursework? How can we together help students overcome their difficulties? We also used teachers' feedback as our guide for program development. A second key ingredient of success, we thought, was time—time for faculty to do the curriculum development necessary for revitalized learning in the classroom. Our administration recognized this and provided release time for faculty to participate in a year-long training program. A third essential element, also encouraged from the start, was a small-group structure for training, a structure that builds on the collegiality and collaboration often lost over time in large academic settings. Finally, we sought to integrate a fourth key element into the training program—a meaningful application of what faculty learn.

The training takes place over an academic year and is undergone on a voluntary basis. Throughout the fall term, program participants (usually about twelve to twenty faculty members) meet weekly in small interdisciplinary work groups (four to six faculty members) under the guidance of a team leader who has also gone through the program. With the strategies in the ISR text as a guide, each faculty member devises classroom applications for the first unit of a course that he or she will teach in the spring. This initial focus on a single unit seems crucial for faculty to acquire a feeling for how integrated reinforcement works. Next, using the target unit as a base, each faculty member develops what is needed to build challenging materials and activities into the rest of the course. The weekly meeting in a small-group setting, with careful feedback from a team leader and ongoing critiques from other group members, ensures that each participant experiences in-depth attention to his or her needs. Through careful work with the team leader and colleagues, faculty discover appropriate places and formats for various tasks and assignments (brief writing assignments, for instance) and determine which assignments they can repeat to facilitate a deeper level of learning. For example, a literature teacher may ask students to write reaction statements after reading a selection, and these can be used in class to start discussion or advance debate. A math teacher may ask students to explain in writing how a homework problem was solved—an assignment designed to reveal conceptual aspects of problem solving. A history teacher may require summaries of historical events or analyses of causes or results. In short, each teacher applies the ISR strategies in different ways, and the team leader and the group help the teacher find ways that feel right—assignments that advance learning in a way that is tailored to particular disciplines, courses, teaching styles, and educational needs.

By the end of the fall term, participants have developed the materials they will need in applying all the strategies to their spring courses. They draw these materials together into a learning guide, which is reproduced for each student's use in the spring, when the teacher tries out the materials in the classroom. In the spring, as faculty teach their courses, they also videotape lessons, annotate their learning guides, meet with their workshop groups to discuss findings, and revise methods and procedures.

By the end of the spring term, each instructor has a field-tested guide that helps students use reading, writing, speaking, and listening as they think critically in relation to various subjects. Beyond their individual use, such guides often serve as valuable resources for other faculty (especially adjuncts) teaching the same courses.

Over 80 percent of LaGuardia's full-time faculty have been trained, and this number includes many department chairpeople. People who have participated in the ISR program say that they internalize the ISR approaches and believe themselves better able to teach their students. They judge the small-group setting as crucial to the program's success. They cite the collaborative exploration of problems, goals, and materials as a key to improving instruction and producing materials that challenge students to think critically and creatively.

Faculty also see improved class performance in areas previously viewed as too difficult for students to grasp. Students selected at random for interviews were five times more likely to enroll in future courses taught in the ISR mode than in courses taught in the traditional mode, and students' responses to particular strategies have been overwhelmingly positive. A self-study conducted by a statistics professor showed significant improvement in student achievement in course sections using ISR methods over achievement in comparable sections of the same course taught by him before the ISR training. Other faculty are pursuing similar self-assessments, and the self-study approach seems a particularly viable one in faculty development efforts built on trust and collegiality.

ISR as a Basis for Collaboration

Curricular Collaboration. The ISR program has spawned intensive curriculum development at our college. Of particular note is a project with our mathematics department in which ISR-trained faculty have collaborated in developing linguistically based materials for widespread use in a basic math course that enrolls large numbers of students. The new materials, which provide contexts for discovery learning of basic mathematical principles, guide students to use writing and discussion to arrive at and advance understanding of important concepts. A recent pilot study of this work has shown a 20 percent increase in the pass rate on a uniform final. Building on this project, we are now developing linguistic strategies to help students explore math concepts in such courses as biology and accounting.

Collaboration with Other Colleges and Graduate Institutions. On the basis of our success with ISR at LaGuardia, other colleges in the City University of New York and elsewhere have adopted and adapted the program with considerable success. ISR programs now exist at CUNY's Bronx Community College, at the State University of New York, Brockport, at Essex County College in Newark, New Jersey, and at Middlesex Community College and Framingham State College, Massachusetts. Workshops on ISR have been offered at many institutions—at Montana State University, at Gonzaga University, Spokane, at Dawson College, Montreal, at Richland College, Dallas, at Laredo State University, and at Western Carolina University, to name just a few. The ISR program is now being offered for graduate credit at Columbia University's Teachers College.

Collaboration with High Schools. The ISR project has provided a context for an exciting new venture in high school/college partnerships. LaGuardia is fortunate to have on its campus the Middle College High School, an innovative and nationally recognized alternative high school. Almost from the start of the ISR program, Middle College teachers have been coparticipants, working alongside their college-level colleagues to find classroom solutions to shared problems.

Almost half of today's high school students go on to some form of postsecondary education—and academic problems travel along with many of them. At LaGuardia, it was clear that high school and college teachers needed to cooperate if students were to learn effectively at each level and move successfully from one level to the next and beyond. High schools prepare students for college, of course, but each kind of institution tends to operate with little knowledge of the other's ways. The ISR partnership, with its integrated perspective on language and learning, has proved important to strengthening the educational chain. Recognizing this, CUNY's

Office of Urban Affairs and the Hearst Foundation enabled us to refine the Middle College/LaGuardia ISR collaboration as a model that could be adapted to the needs of other LaGuardia feeder high schools. The LaGuardia/Middle College partnership is now widening its focus and launching a new initiative, which has teachers from both levels engaged in exploring the scope of general education within and between the institutions.

Conclusion

The ISR program and its collaborative ventures have been made possible over the years by the care and support of LaGuardia's administration, as well as by the generosity and encouragement of the U.S. Office of Education (under Title III), the New York State Education Department, the City University of New York's Office of Urban Affairs, and the Hearst Foundation. ISR was named a "project of excellence" in a statewide competition cosponsored by the Two-Year College Development Center and the Grants Administration Bureau of the New York State Education Department. The National Association for Remedial/Developmental Studies in Postsecondary Education awarded its first annual John Champaigne Memorial Award to LaGuardia's developmental program (of which ISR is an integral part), citing LaGuardia's program as representing the best of current practice in the field.

ISR has demonstrated its power to create dynamic faculty communities dedicated to serving varied student constituencies. This experience seems to indicate the type of faculty development program that can play an important role in addressing the major educational problems in schools and colleges today. The ISR collaborative ventures provide faculty with the time and environment to rethink and rework curricula. Teachers who come out of the program are no longer depleted by isolated struggle. They are revitalized and rededicated. In these small educational communities, teachers together discover approaches that help students find something in language: not a wall, but a door to learning and knowledge.

JoAnn Romeo Anderson is a professor and ISR project director at LaGuardia Community College. She also serves as special assistant for academic instructional affairs in the office of the vice-president and dean of faculty.

Nora Eisenberg is a professor in LaGuardia's English department. She has been an associate director and trainer of ISR for the past ten years.

Harvey S. Wiener is associate dean of academic affairs at CUNY Central. He has been an associate director and trainer of ISR for the past ten years.

This WAC program sends English department writing consultants into eight major technical and allied-health programs.

The Writing Consultancy Project

Christine M. Godwin

It started out very small, very casual. Over coffee, an engineering instructor said to a writing teacher, "I got this terrible batch of reports from my Engineering II students. Will you take a look at them and tell me what to do?" Nine years later, Orange County Community College's Writing Consultancy Project is a WAC program that has evolved to meet the complex needs of students and faculty in eight technical and allied-health programs.

As it begins the new academic year, this project is a model of a combination (English department–administered, content area–based) WAC program that channels the community college's energies and resources to prepare students in the classroom and on the job, encourage writing-intensive technical and allied-health courses, and develop faculty in the vocational areas and in English. Its success is based on the continuing joint commitment of faculty. It illustrates how a community college can creatively meet the needs of its varied constituencies.

Critical Components

An examination of the Writing Consultancy Project's critical components illustrates how such a structure can serve the immediate needs of vocational programs. Its model can also be the jumping-off point for institutions that are ready to develop their own uniquely tailored WAC programs.

Key Goals. In the very practical, needs-specific vocational areas, product and service quality and dependability are carefully regulated and monitored, and projects are often funded after their documentation has been examined. Technical and allied-health professionals must therefore think and write carefully, clearly, and accurately. They must produce good written

NEW DIRECTIONS FOR COMMUNITY COLLEGES, no. 73, Spring 1991 © Jossey-Bass Inc., Publishers

products, but they must also have processes and approaches for tackling changing documentation demands on the job. The Writing Consultancy Project's main goals are to teach students how to transfer and apply key writing skills to vocational situations, help them develop an ongoing process for coping with changing situations in the classroom and the workplace, and give them hands-on experience in types of on-the-job writing and environments. In the process, students take an active role and, through their work with the various drafts of their technical reports, they develop their own sense of what is happening. One faculty-related goal is to develop technical and writing instructors' ability to teach writing and reinforce technical instruction in these situations.

Basic Project Structure. At the request of vocational programs and course instructors, English department writing consultants work with faculty and students in technical and allied-health courses. The instructors teach lessons and develop materials that help the students transfer and apply key writing skills to already required documentation such as laboratory reports, notebooks, summaries, technical proposals, clinical notes, treatment plans, and nursing-care plans. They do this through credit-bearing technical writing modules, which are prerequisites for designated vocational courses; team-taught writing workshops within vocational course sequences; special large- and small-group presentations; one-to-one conferencing; and supervised work in the project's computer-equipped Technical/Medical Writing Laboratory. All these efforts foster both a product and a process approach to writing across the vocational curriculum.

Sample Program Plans. Like the programs in occupational therapy and physical therapy assisting, the program in electrical technology has attached a writing consultancy–based technical writing module to the freshman Electricity I and sophomore Research Project in Electricity courses. Through team teaching, the writing consultant and the technology instructor work with students on the same writing projects (laboratory reports, notebooks, summaries, and formal reports). In addition to a twenty-minute workshop at the beginning of the weekly electricity lab, the consultant confers with students individually on rough and final drafts of their weekly summaries and supervises their writing in the Technical/Medical Writing Laboratory. In the individual conferences, students take command of their texts by asking questions of the consultants, and these questions direct and drive the student-teacher interchange. These exchanges also help students discover what they do or do not know and what they are or are not sure of in technical knowledge. Final drafts are graded by both instructors.

In the four-semester program in nursing, a writing consultant and a nursing instructor teach sixteen specially designed documentation workshops within the Nursing I–IV course sequence. Each workshop is built around a nursing-documentation situation and specific writing skills. Students write and check their nursing notes during the workshops. All materials have been edited by the nursing department faculty. In the Engineering I–II sequence, the writing consultant and the technical instructor use a two-semester series of class lectures and individual conferences that culminate in a formal technical proposal.

Sample Lesson/Workshop. The joint approach is mirrored in individual lessons like the one on writing patient-interaction reports for occupational therapy. After planning an initial two-session lesson and creating materials, the instructor and the writing consultant explain the writing situation to freshman students, incorporating both the allied-health and the writing-thinking perspective. They then ask the students to view a videotaped patient-therapist interaction, and they discuss the observed details, the potential conclusions, and the methods and skills for the write-up. Students then view the tape again and write their rough drafts at computers. After analyzing these, the two instructors meet again with the students, using examples from the drafts to illustrate how the writing skills must be applied. Students then have individual conferences, revise at the computers, and turn in final drafts, which are evaluated by both instructors. A similar sequence is used for specific courses and reports in the physical therapy assisting and medical laboratory technology programs.

Teamwork. The Writing Consultancy experience illustrates the vital necessity of collaborative effort between instructors. This continuing interaction is crucial to students' successful transfer and application of writing skills to vocational situations. To ensure that instructor and consultant work well together, the Writing Consultancy has followed these guidelines:

1. Technical and allied-health instructors request consultants.
2. Consultants are specially selected writing instructors who want to work in such a situation.
3. The technical instructor is the technical expert who leads the consultant.
4. The consultant suggests appropriate writing strategies, which both instructors agree to.
5. Consultants sit in on each session of the technical or allied-health course during the first application, and only as needed thereafter.

Support Facility and Materials. Although it is an English department program, the Writing Consultancy Project is decentralized. Its consultants work in the vocational classrooms and labs. Whenever possible, they have desks in those areas and supervise students' writing in the Technical/Medical Writing Laboratory. All computerized materials and print handouts are specially created for, adapted to, and illustrated by the specific writing situations and samples from each program. These are also updated as vocational needs demand.

Funding. Initially, there were no regular funding sources for the project. In its first four years, the project was a voluntary round of faculty workshops, the Interdisciplinary Reading-Writing Project. Faculty donated their time; the institution provided meeting space and clerical and publication support. In the next stage, the Writing Consultancy Project was created, largely through the joint efforts of the English and technology departments. The institution redefined the writing consultants' teaching load during a two-semester experiment with the courses in engineering and electrical technology. When that proved successful, and when three departments requested credit-bearing Technical Writing Modules, tuition dollars began to support the program. Later, when the Technical/Medical Writing Laboratory was developed, a regular lab fee was added.

New York State then awarded four Vocational Education Act grants to the Writing Consultancy Project for further development of the Technical/Medical Writing Laboratory. The State University of New York underwrote the development of the sixteen writing workshops for the program in nursing through a faculty grant for improvement of undergraduate instruction. Other grant proposals are being planned.

Outreach. To extend Writing Across the Vocational Curriculum and maintain an informed outlook on technical and allied-health needs, the Writing Consultancy Project is involved in three outreach activities. Its consultants plan and implement training programs for the college's Institute for Business, Industry and Government. They sit on the advisory boards of that institute and of selected vocational programs. They report regularly to other advisory boards and present workshops to clinical proctors in allied-health programs. They regularly participate in each vocational program's reaccreditation. With their technical and allied-health partners, writing consultants also present information about the Writing Consultancy Project at state, regional, and national conferences.

Critical Perspectives

A WAC program is not, ultimately, assessed according to its components; rather, it is judged by its continuing ability to meet its clients' needs—and, by extension, those of the community college's constituency. Looking backward and forward, the Writing Consultancy Project has assessed its success through students' and faculty's evaluations and responses, accrediting agencies' assessments, and honors and awards.

Here is one freshman's comment during a late-semester conference about his rough-draft lab summary: "You know, when I went back to check this, I realized that my opening sentence is lousy. I can't word it because I don't understand what the lab was about. So I talked to Mr. R. about Thevenin's theorem again. Now look at how I rewrote it." That is a student's own evaluation of his success and the program's. It is reflected in the class's grades, in the quality of their rough and final drafts, and in their comments in their journals and on evaluation forms. They all say the same thing: they may not love writing, but they understand its importance in the mastery of content and in preparation for jobs. They cite their improved ability to apply writing skills to documentation tasks. Graduates have written letters and answered reaccreditation surveys in similar ways; in fact, they encourage enlargement of the program.

The English department's writing consultants have high praise for this approach in their course evaluations. They continue asking to work in the program. They meet more and more regularly with their technical and allied-health partners. Those instructors also continue to remain in the program. They become increasingly involved in talking about writing during the student-teacher conferences, and they spread the word to colleagues in other fields.

Accrediting agencies have lauded this WAC program in their formal reports. Employers, technical and allied-health advisory boards, clinical proctors, and field supervisors have sent letters documenting students' increased writing skills. Finally, granting agencies have continued to fund the project. The Writing Consultancy Project has been featured in national magazines, and it was selected as the outstanding college-level vocational education program by the New York State Department of Education.

The critical challenge to the Writing Consultancy Project, and to any other WAC program, is this: it must remain fluid, adapting itself to the changing needs of its vocational clients, to the community college's constituents and mission, and to the industrial and allied-health communities. That means that its foundation must be evolution, responsiveness, and a great deal of listening and learning. When a WAC program is built on that foundation, it works.

Christine M. Godwin, professor of English, supervises the Writing Consultancy Project and coordinates the Technical/Medical Writing Laboratory at Orange County Community College. She is coauthor of Writing Skills for Nurses *(Reston, 1983).*

The Community Communication Corps, a partnership between education and business in the promotion of communication skills, provides the opportunity for a real-world educational experience that is exciting and rewarding.

Beyond Writing Across the Curriculum: The Community Communication Corps

Stanley P. Witt

The Community Communication Corps reflects a new way of thinking about the educational process at Pima Community College (PCC), yet the roots of the corps go back more than eight years to when a faculty survey at PCC's East Campus indicated a need to improve students' literacy. Accordingly, the dean established an advisory committee to lay plans for a WAC program. The following spring, a WAC coordinator, appointed from the writing department, recruited eleven faculty, held workshops, and launched the project. While a follow-up survey confirmed the value of the WAC undertaking, it also underscored the need for integration of a second language skill. After some debate, the WAC advisory committee decided to add a Speaking Across the Curriculum (SAC) component, mainly because of the practical, real-world applications of speech, particularly in the job market.

Establishing a Multischool WAC/SAC

In the meantime, exploratory cooperative efforts had begun with key people from the communication departments at two feeder high schools. After several sharing meetings, plans emerged for a joint WAC/SAC venture. Among the eventual fruit of these labors was a substantial three-year Fund for the Improvement of Postsecondary Education (FIPSE) grant enabling the expansion of the WAC/SAC project into a multischool enterprise that encompassed the three PCC campuses and five feeder high schools, providing advisory support from the English and speech departments at the University of Arizona.

The promotional strategy of this FIPSE project embodied several key aims. One was the education of faculty and administrators concerning the intimate relationship between language skills (such as writing and speaking), on the one hand, and thinking, learning, and expressing (communicating) thinking and learning, on the other. A second key element of our strategy—one characterized by Richardson, Fisk, and Okun (1983) as essential to the success of literacy programs—was the cultivation of an attitude that would view literacy as a campuswide responsibility. Responsibility for literacy had to be embraced on a campuswide basis because the sparse number of required writing and speech courses was insufficient to remediate years of skills deficiencies, as reflected in students' work at every level from middle school through college.

Our strategy paid off in measurable improvements in students' proficiency levels as, over the next three years, the local secondary and postsecondary educational community imbibed massive doses of WAC and SAC. The undertaking also made valuable headway in articulating tentative exit standards in writing and in speech for high school seniors and community college sophomores, our goal being to facilitate students' ability to transfer from one level of education to the next.

Broadening the Concept

Although we were gratified by these results, we began to realize that the project did not go far enough to meet the needs of students whose primary educational goal was to prepare themselves to pursue careers. Classroom activities devised by participating faculty were usually limited to the writing-to-learn or speaking-to-express-learning variety. WAC students, for example, prepared journals, interactive logs, or "thinkbooks," many of which activities are described by Gere (1985). Thus, while there was much emphasis on the importance of writing skills in an academic setting, little attention was given to the real-world application of these skills or to the public (as opposed to the private) function of communication skills—a recurrent criticism of WAC programs (see Chapter Four).

Moreover, the project did not advance such career-essential communication skills as reading, listening, and critical thinking. Critical thinking is relevant to literacy projects because today it is often used as a measure of literacy (see Brookfield, 1987; Hirsch, 1987; Meyers, 1986; Richardson, Fisk, and Okun, 1983; Tuman, 1987). Again, the project did not reach far enough into the educational system to engage the participation of middle schools, the point in our educational system at which integrative learning begins to fragment.

Finally, the project was too narrow in defining literacy as merely a campuswide responsibility. Literacy must be promoted by the real-world community, not just by educators in the make-believe world of academia.

The community is, after all, both a contributor to the literacy crisis and a beneficiary of the crisis's remediation. Putting this argument aside, and looking at the problem from a practical standpoint, we can see that we need the active support of the community simply because the crisis has grown too formidable for schools alone to remediate.

Starting a Pilot Project

Undoubtedly the most distinguishing feature of the corps is the involvement of the business community in the promotion of communication skills. The idea for this resource—new, exciting, and abundant—came quite by accident, when a language-arts coordinator in a Phoenix-area high school district told us about a very successful project that was advancing several communication skills among the employees of a local bank. Expanding on this concept, and utilizing our WAC/SAC connections with feeder schools, we began to recruit volunteer faculty and representatives from business for a local project.

Referred to as business partners in education (or BPEs), corps participants from business and industry represented nearly the whole range of Tucson's activity—large corporations, small businesses, wholesalers, retailers, manufacturing firms, public agencies, and city and county government. BPEs either volunteered their time or received release time from their places of employment. In one sense, the commitment of these participants seemed to embody a happy, compromise solution to the contradiction that Bellah and others (1985) see as a persistent trait of the American businessperson: the dichotomy between the impulse for self-reliant individualism and the urge for community service.

BPEs were not expected to be specialists in communication skills, but rather people with reasonable facility in one or more of the five designated skills: reading, writing, speaking, listening, and critical thinking. They were paired with faculty across the disciplines from PCC's three campuses and with volunteer teachers from feeder high schools and middle schools. About half the feeder schools had large minority populations. These were the schools where literacy levels seemed lowest and where career-oriented students were in greatest abundance.

BPEs and teachers, known as T-teams (teaching teams), met in workshops with communication-skills specialists to prepare units for classroom presentation. The job of the specialists was to provide resource material and suggestions for pedagogical effectiveness. As expected, the most successful units turned out to be those in which collaboration with specialists was greatest. It is also important to note that the greatest successes occurred in T-teams in which BPEs were not merely guest speakers but became integrated into classroom activities, participating in discussion sessions and assisting in the evaluation of relevant assignments.

The diversity of T-team units proved to be extraordinary, involving role playing, mock interviews, written scenarios, oral summaries, nonverbal communication, résumés, formal speeches, and impromptu debates. In all, there was a good deal of emphasis on problem-solving strategies and exercises in critical thinking, with an occasional activity concentrating on critical listening or on critical reading.

Most T-teams attempted to balance what Richardson, Fisk, and Okun (1983) have described as academic literacy (needed for scholarly and literary achievement) with functional literacy (required for real-world success)— that is, the T-teams used communication-skills activities that had discernible relevance to course content but were grounded in the working world and underscored the real-world necessity of the skills being modeled. The functional value of literacy was also enhanced in some classes, where BPEs, assisting in the evaluation of relevant assignments, stressed—often to the astonishment of students—the real-world necessity of correct spelling and punctuation, effective organization of ideas, clarity, and polish. Corps teachers especially welcomed this added emphasis on functional literacy. As one high school math teacher observed, using real-world activities heightened her students' interest and awareness: "Textbook situations are not adequate preparations for the future."

Altering Students' Attitudes

What had impressed us most about the Phoenix-based literacy project in the bank was its success in improving students' attitudes toward communication skills. Our experience in the corps was similarly gratifying. For corps teachers, the old adage "Seeing is believing" took on new and refreshing meaning, a meaning vividly reflected in changed attitudes. In fact, T-teams were often able to effect attitudinal changes in one or two classroom visits, changes that teachers alone had been unable to inspire in years of futile preachments. It was also discovered that when students' attitudes about communication skills underwent favorable change, such change enhanced learning. In short, the real value of having BPEs in the classroom lay not in their "teaching" the teachers' classes but in their reshaping the students' attitudes toward the importance of communication skills.

Project evaluations confirmed the beneficial effects of BPEs in the classrooms. In all, there were twenty-four T-teams and more than six hundred students. Eighty-one percent of the participating students described their learning experience with the BPEs as substantially worthwhile, 11 percent characterized the experience as worthwhile, 5 percent had no opinion, and 3 percent responded negatively. Virtually all the participating faculty proclaimed the positive value of the approach, and the majority of the BPEs signed up for class visits during the next semester.

Funding the Corps

Funding the corps was inexpensive and uncomplicated. There was little outlay connected with classroom activities; a few dollars here and there for materials and duplication were sufficient. Most project funds, furnished jointly by the executive deans at PCC's three campuses, went for recruitment breakfasts and for stipends to coordinators, workshop facilitators, and tutors. The East Campus, where the corps originated, provided additional revenue in the form of release time for the corps director. For the future, the PCC district headquarters has not only included corps activities in an incentive program for faculty development but also has pledged stipends for one high school coordinator and one middle school coordinator. As is often the case, local high school and middle school budgets have been too cramped to supply financial assistance beyond occasional release time for teachers.

Meeting the Future

Although the corps is not yet one year old, it is bearing healthy fruit. For instance, the corps is helping to foster good community relations, particularly among the community's schools and businesses. It is helping to dispel ingrained prejudices and traditional antagonisms between educators and businesspeople. It is inspiring teachers with ideas for newer and more effective classroom techniques. Almost without exception, teachers who participated in the corps pilot project expressed an excitement about the educational process that they had not felt in a long time. They liked the newness and freshness of an approach that strives to maintain pedagogical integrity while interacting organically with the community. Of course, the community's students were the principal beneficiaries of corps activities. A good many students learned, from BPEs whom they seemed quite willing to believe, the crucial importance of communication proficiency as a condition for survival in the world outside. Students have also received valuable coaching in developing techniques designed to improve their academic and functional literacy levels.

There is yet another aspect of learning that corps activities enhanced, an aspect that, according to Zwerling (1986), goes to the very heart of the community college mission: in order to meet the challenge of the future, students must be taught the value of lifelong learning as a means to an abundant life. Implicit in the corps approach is a belief in the importance of developing skills that facilitate life's many transitions, whether from one educational institution to the next or from one career to another.

Whether the corps will become a permanent fixture in the local educational system remains an open question, but its survival for the immediate future seems assured. Additional feeder schools, businesses, and public agencies have signed up for the coming year, ensuring that the number of students affected by corps activities will increase to several thousand. An important goal for the third year will be the establishment in the community of an autonomous "booster club" whose function will be maintaining an active roster of BPEs to fuel the large network of "corps clusters" that will be operating throughout the Tucson area.

For the next few years, the corps hopes to play a significant role in preparing students to meet the twenty-first century with real-world education. In a meaningful way, the corps meets the challenge for greater community outreach and involvement in the educational process, including the promotion of communication skills.

References

Bellah, R. N., Madsen, R., Sullivan, W. M., Swidler, A., and Tipton, S. M. *Habits of the Heart: Individualism and Commitment in American Life*. Berkeley: University of California Press, 1985.

Brookfield, S. D. *Developing Critical Thinkers: Challenging Adults to Explore Alternative Ways of Thinking and Acting*. San Francisco: Jossey-Bass, 1987.

Gere, A. R. (ed.). *Roots in the Sawdust: Writing to Learn Across the Disciplines*. Urbana, Ill.: National Council of Teachers of English, 1985.

Hirsch, E. D., Jr. *Cultural Literacy: What Every American Needs to Know*. Boston: Houghton Mifflin, 1987.

Meyers, C. *Teaching Students to Think Critically: A Guide for Faculty in All Disciplines*. San Francisco: Jossey-Bass, 1986.

Richardson, R. C., Jr., Fisk, E. C., and Okun, M. A. *Literacy in the Open-Access College*. San Francisco: Jossey-Bass, 1983.

Tuman, M. C. *A Preface to Literacy: An Inquiry into Pedagogy, Practice, and Process*. Tuscaloosa: University of Alabama Press, 1987.

Zwerling, L. S. "Lifelong Learning: A New Form of Tracking." In L. S. Zwerling (ed.), *The Community College and Its Critics*. San Francisco: Jossey-Bass, 1986.

Stanley P. Witt is chair of writing and Humanities at the East Campus of Pima Community College and director of the Community Communication Corps.

An annotated bibliography presents ERIC documents and journal articles on Writing Across the Curriculum programs in community colleges.

Sources and Information

Dana Nicole Williams

Writing Across the Curriculum (WAC) programs originated at colleges and universities in the United States during the mid 1970s in response to a perceived deficiency in students' writing and thinking abilities. Since then, programs have been established at public and private two- and four-year colleges and universities in all parts of the country.

Study after study have pointed to the benefits of successful WAC programs, both for faculty and students. For students, these programs strengthen critical-thinking skills and writing ability while also promoting overall literacy and active participation in learning. For faculty members, the programs address such problems as disciplinary isolation and burnout while improving curricular coherence and institutionwide morale.

This chapter provides an annotated bibliography of recent ERIC literature on WAC programs at community and junior colleges. The ERIC documents listed here can be obtained from the ERIC Document Reproduction Service, 3900 Wheeler Ave., Alexandria, Virginia 22304-6409 (Tel.: 800-277-3742). The journal articles cited in this bibliography are *not* available from ERIC and must be obtained through regular library channels.

Background Information

The following materials provide background information on WAC programs. A history of the WAC movement and a rationale for the implementation of this approach are offered in many documents.

Adams, B., Smith, M., Bodino, A., and Bissell, O. "Writing for Learning: How to Achieve Total College Commitment." Papers presented at the annual convention of the American Association of Community and Junior Colleges, San Diego, Calif., April 14-17, 1985. 38 pp. (ED 258 666) Various aspects of the Writing Across the Curriculum program at Somerset County College (SCC) in New Jersey are discussed in four papers. Smith traces the program's development. Bodino looks at writing as a learning tool, the purposes of writing, the place of writing throughout the curriculum, correctness in writing, and the role of critics and evaluators in the writing process. Bissell describes SCC's three-year project to encourage faculty's use of WAC in the classroom. Adams underscores the importance of consensus on standards for college-level writing.

Bertch, J. "Writing for Learning: Starting a Writing Across the Curriculum Program in the Community College." Paper presented at the Conference on High School–College Articulation in Writing, Tempe, Ariz., April 19–20, 1985. 11 pp. (ED 256 387) This paper on the steps involved in initiating a community college WAC program begins by listing three basic premises: more learning is achieved when writing is involved; learning to write involves learning to manage and coordinate the component skills of writing while performing real writing tasks; and writing teaches students to actively touch the content of a class. Implementation begins with a clear statement of the rationale for the WAC program and its goals, followed by the enlistment of faculty and administrative support. Support is further developed through workshops for teachers, on such topics as notetaking, class logs, study guides, writing assignments, essay tests, and conference evaluations.

Holladay, J. *Institutional Project Grant: A Report on Research into Writing Across the Curriculum Projects.* Monroe, Mich.: Monroe County Community College, 1987. 80 pp. (ED 298 995) Drawing on a literature review, telephone interviews with community college writing directors in Michigan, and a survey of faculty members at Monroe County Community College (MCCC), this report assesses the status of WAC programs in community colleges and offers recommendations for implementing a writing center–based WAC program at MCCC. After defining WAC and reviewing the literature on the benefits and drawbacks of four WAC models, the report analyzes the applicability of these models for MCCC. Results of a survey of MCCC faculty are presented, indicating that an overwhelming majority of the college's students have writing problems in such areas as organization, supporting an idea, coherence, grammar, punctuation, spelling, vocabulary, and proofreading.

Hughes-Wiener, G., and Martin, G. R. "Results of Instructional Research in a Writing Across the Curriculum Staff Development Program." Paper presented at the annual meeting of the American Educational Research Association, San Francisco, March 27-31, 1989. 20 pp. (ED 305 967)
This report assesses the effectiveness of a three-year WAC staff development program undertaken by the Minnesota Community College System. On the basis of faculty interviews, student and faculty surveys, holistic ratings of student papers, and essay exams in four subject areas, the report considers the effects of the WAC program on students' writing quality and mastery of course content. Study findings revealed that compositions collected at the end of the term received significantly better ratings than those collected at the beginning, although factors other than WAC instruction may have contributed to the improvement. A slight positive correlation was found between students' cumulative writing experience and writing quality, attitudes toward writing, and comprehension of subject material.

Ulisse, P. *Writing Across the Curriculum.* Stratford, Conn.: Housatonic Community College, 1988. 51 pp. (ED 310 828)
Designed to provide information to Housatonic Community College administrators on the status of WAC programs, this document presents a historical overview of the WAC movement, strategies for program implementation, and examples of WAC programs currently in existence across the nation. General suggestions are offered for teaching WAC courses, such as using formal papers, essay exams, and written homework assignments. Specific techniques are also presented for science, math, business, social science, and non-English humanities courses. After describing twelve successful WAC programs, the author lists steps for implementing and evaluating WAC programs. The appendices include sample writing assignments, course syllabi, and a 176-item bibliography.

Sample Programs

Several different types of WAC programs have emerged, adapted to each college's specific needs. The following are a sample of the variations.

Bertch, J. "Assuring Course Availability: A Writing-Based System for Independent Study." Paper presented at the annual conference of the Pacific Western Division of the Community College Humanities Association, Seattle, Wash., Nov. 14-16, 1985. 21 pp. (ED 269 788)
In response to difficulties in offering advanced-level courses with low enrollments, this paper proposes the development of a bank of writing-based advanced courses to be offered for independent study. The steps in devel-

oping the course bank are discussed, including planning course content, writing unit goals, and selecting the forms of presentation. Students are required to read study guides, take notes, annotate and underline readings, paraphrase and summarize, keep learning logs, write papers, and take essay tests.

Bertch, J. "Writing for Learning in the Community College." Paper presented at the Models for Excellence Conference, Cedar Rapids, Iowa, May 30–June 1, 1985. 15 pp. (ED 256 458)

After tracing trends in the WAC movement, this paper compares two forms of WAC: a more traditional, formally structured approach, based on writing as a discipline; and programs based on a more flexible view of writing as a thinking process fundamental to understanding. This second approach, termed *writing for learning*, consists of multiple activities, all designed to lead students to interact with the content of their courses in ways that result in increased learning. Students write in and out of class, by themselves and in groups. Sometimes their writing is cued, and sometimes it is self-designed. The implementation of this approach at South Mountain Community College in Arizona is described.

Booher, S. C. *A Report on the Tutorial Outreach Model for Reading and Writing Across the Curriculum at Los Medanos College*. Pittsburgh, Calif.: Los Medanos College, 1982. 253 pp. (ED 221 252)

This document outlines the peer-tutoring approach to Writing Across the Curriculum used by Los Medanos (LMC) in California. In 1980, LMC began a two-year project to train full-time faculty to supervise, direct, and support peer tutors. Semester-length faculty seminars, taught by language-arts faculty, covered such topics as how to select a tutor, how to screen classes for literacy problems, and how to reinforce good reading and writing habits. Tutor-training classes were also offered by the language-arts faculty. Students who received tutoring had higher grades and retention rates than students selected for tutoring who did not receive it.

Holladay, J. *Monroe County Community College Writing Across the Curriculum: Annual Report, 1988–89*. Monroe, Mich.: Monroe County Community College, 1989. 27 pp. (ED 310 820)

This evaluative report focuses on two aspects of Monroe County Community College's WAC program: its writing center, and the provision of peer tutoring by instructor-nominated writing fellows. Using statistics on increased use of the center, evaluation of the fellows program by students who worked with peer tutors, survey responses from participating faculty members, and program evaluations by the tutors, the report highlights the benefits of WAC for faculty, writing fellows, college administrators, and students.

Landsburg, D., and Witt, S. "Writing Across the Curriculum: One Small Step." *Innovation Abstracts*, 1984, *6* (13). 4 pp. (ED 248 922)

A description is provided of the WAC program at the East Campus of Pima Community College (PCC). At PCC, faculty in all disciplines are asked to get involved in the WAC program, and those who participate are paid a one-time fee of $100 for their efforts. After participating faculty develop writing assignments according to prescribed criteria, students complete the assignments and submit their papers to their course instructors. The instructors turn the papers over to "collateral graders"—writing instructors who grade the papers for mechanics, mark errors, and indicate whether the papers pass or must be rewritten. Then the course instructors grade the passing papers for content. The use of collateral graders has several advantages: the students receive writing feedback on grammar, spelling, punctuation, and usage from experts; awareness of the need for campuswide writing standards is generated; and student-teacher negotiation concerning the importance of writing skills is reduced.

McLeod, S. H. (ed.). *Strengthening Programs for Writing Across the Curriculum.* New Directions for Teaching and Learning, no. 36. San Francisco: Jossey-Bass, 1988.

This volume offers guidelines for developing and sustaining WAC programs. Issues faced by WAC program coordinators are addressed, including how to develop and maintain programs, ensure continued funding, and conduct meaningful program evaluation. Specific guidelines for establishing WAC programs at community colleges, as well as an annotated reference list of WAC programs across the country, are included.

Martin-Jordan, D., and Moorhead, M. "Writing Across the Curriculum: The Mentor Project." *Teaching English in the Two-Year College*, 1989, *16* (2), 99–103.

Moorehead, M., and Martin-Jordan, D. *Eastfield College "Writing Across the Curriculum": The Mentor Project.* Mesquite, Tex.: Eastfield College, 1987. 11 pp. (ED 283 540)

These articles describe Eastfield College's WAC Mentor Project, an effort initiated in 1986 to involve the entire Eastfield faculty in the improvement of students' writing. English faculty serve as mentors to all other faculty and help them develop writing assignments and essay tests. They also teach them grading techniques for written work. The 1987 article describes the phases in the development of the project, which included interviews with English and non-English faculty, an informational workshop for interested faculty, and a mechanism by which English faculty assisted their colleagues in the development of writing tasks for particular courses.

Nakamura, C., Fearrien, R., and Hershinow, S. "Writing to Learn: Writing Across the Curriculum at Kapiolani Community College." Papers presented at the Pacific Western Division Conference of the Community College Humanities Association, San Diego, Calif., November 8–10, 1984. 14 pp. (ED 252 252)

Three papers focus on WAC at Kapiolani Community College in Hawaii. Nakamura provides an overview of WAC programs offered across the country, discusses the need for WAC in terms of the decline in students' writing ability, and highlights recent findings on the nature and function of writing. Fearrien traces the history of Kapiolani's writing program and examines the assumptions and procedures that guided the program's development. Hershinow offers guidelines for curriculum development based on the assumption that writing is a continuous and inescapable part of every student's career, requiring continual practice in all spheres of the curriculum.

Walter, J. A. "Paired Classes: Write to Learn and Learn to Write." Paper presented at the annual meeting of the Community College Humanities Association, Kalamazoo, Mich., October 5–6, 1984. 8 pp. (ED 248 933)

After noting WAC's role in helping students learn to learn and improve their attitudes about writing, this paper describes the use of a paired-classes model of WAC at Sinclair Community College (Ohio). Students had the option of signing up for specific sections of a writing course paired with a humanities course. The humanities course was structured according to mastery-learning techniques in easily manageable units. At the end of each mastery-learning unit, the student was required to produce a written composition. Students worked on these assignments and others in the writing course.

Generating Writing Assignments

The following documents provide sample writing assignments that can be adapted for use in content-area classes, or offer guidelines for developing such assignments.

Ingham, Z. (ed.). *Writing Across the Curriculum Sample Assignments, 1986–1987.* Tucson, Ariz.: Pima Community College, 1986. 134 pp. (ED 296 743)

This booklet provides fifty sample writing assignments prepared for thirty-eight nonwriting courses taught at Pima Community College. Three types of assignments are represented: short, one- to five-page papers, which allow students to use instructors' feedback in producing improved papers as the course progresses; formal papers, ranging from five to twenty pages, which require students to conduct research, synthesize information, and provide references; and interactive learning logs in which students freely respond to class discussions and reading assignments. Examples of students' writing, grading criteria, and standards of composition are also included.

Killingsworth, J. (ed.). *Designing Writing Assignments for Vocational-Technical Courses.* Lubbock, Tex.: Texas Tech University, 1988. 202 pp. (ED 298 331) The twenty-seven articles in this six-part guide provide information on developing and implementing writing instruction in two-year technical and vocational courses. The sections of the handbook focus on (1) general concerns, such as evaluating students' writing and using word processors; (2) the balance between world-of-work writing and writing-as-learning assignments; (3) sample writing assignments designed to reinforce course content in nursing, agricultural marketing, automotive-engine repair, unarmed-defense tactics, office procedures, and dental hygiene; (4) sample assignments to promote the accomplishment of professional goals in such fields as fashion promotion, high technology, advertising, management, and public administration; (5) ways of fitting writing assignments into course plans; and (6) preparing students and instructors for Writing Across the Curriculum.

Preston, J. *Writing Across the Curriculum. Some Questions and Answers and a Series of Eleven Writing Projects for Instructors of the General Education Core Courses: Energy and the Natural Environment, Humanities, Individual in Transition, and Social Environment.* Miami, Fla.: Miami–Dade Community College, 1982. 114 pp. (ED 256 414)
Eleven writing projects for students are suggested: a diagnostic writing assignment, a summary of the main content of a day's presentation, a written explanation of some aspect of coursework, a short report on an out-of-class activity, a summary of a reading assignment, a book review, a response to an audio-visual presentation, an essay, a research paper, an essay test, and a journal. Suggested techniques and sample handouts are also provided, along with answers to questions on the use of screening tests, applications of the eleven projects, the use of handouts, and the importance of sentence form, punctuation, and spelling in grading.

Simmons, J. M. (ed.). *The Shortest Distance to Learning: A Guidebook to Writing Across the Curriculum.* Los Angeles: Los Angeles Community College District, 1983. 62 pp. (ED 241 073)
This guidebook provides materials to help teachers in a variety of subject areas integrate writing and learning in the classroom. The booklet begins by addressing a number of common concerns that instructors have about teaching writing in their courses. The remaining chapters offer guidance on the use of learning logs (journals in which students take class notes and also record their thoughts on films, lectures, and so on), writing assignments, assignment sequences, and essay tests.

Storlie, E. F., and Barwise, M. *Asking Good Questions, Getting Good Writing: A Teacher's Handbook on Writing Across the Curriculum at Minneapolis Community College.* Minneapolis, Minn.: Minneapolis Community College, 1985. 104 pp. (ED 210 284)
This handbook provides teachers with effective, efficient, and practical suggestions for crafting good writing assignments in content-area classrooms. The chapters in the handbook discuss ways in which teachers can save time and energy in assigning and grading writing, provide examples of writing assignments for promoting learning, and discuss principles to help teachers ask questions that demand thinking. The book also suggests alternatives to traditional term papers, reviews the role of classroom discussions and other activities in preparing students to succeed as writers, and recommends time-saving ways of marking papers.

Faculty Participation

Often the most important aspect of beginning a WAC program is recruiting interested faculty to participate. The following documents focus on ways that community college leaders involve faculty in WAC programs.

Bertch, J. *The Maricopa Writing Project, Summer 1987: Project Report.* Phoenix, Ariz.: Maricopa County Community College, 1987. 11 pp. (ED 286 565)
This case study evaluates two faculty workshops held in the summer of 1987 by the Maricopa Writing Project to encourage faculty involvement in WAC programs. Activities in these workshops included researching innovative methods of integrating writing instruction into the disciplines, forming interest groups for in-depth study of such topics as writing for learning and writing and thinking, adding a significant writing assignment to courses currently taught, and making a brief presentation on a successful writing assignment.

Bilson, B., and Ryan, K. J. (eds.). *Inside English,* 1983-84, *11* (1-4). 42 pp. (ED 288 573)

Bilson, B., and Woodroof, B. (eds.). *Inside English,* 1985-86, *13* (1-4). 52 pp. (ED 288 575)
Designed primarily for English faculty at California community colleges, *Inside English* includes articles on instructional innovations in teaching remedial writing, literature courses, and freshman composition, as well as articles on major curricular, administrative, and employment issues in the field. These two entire volumes of the journal include a number of articles on Writing Across the Curriculum, including "Writing Across the Curriculum: A Unique Value for Learning," by Nancy H. Nadeau; "Writing for Learning: Programs and Ideas," by Trish Geddes; "Writing Across the

Curriculum: Raising Student Literacy AND Faculty Morale," by Susan H. McLeod; and "Teaching Teachers: Resistance and Writing Across the Curriculum," by Judith R. Hert.

Copeland, J. S. (ed.). *Essays Grown from a Writing Across the Curriculum Institute at Indian Hills Community College: Fostering Cooperation and Cohesion in Writing Instruction.* Indian Hills, Iowa: Indian Hills Community College, 1987. 56 pp. (ED 294 182)

This collection of fourteen essays describes methods of using writing as a learning tool across various disciplines. The workshop from which these essays were derived examined current theories and research on writing instruction, methods of using writing in various disciplines, ways of fostering cooperation and cohesion in writing instruction among instructors from different subject areas, and the personal writing development of the instructors. The essays focus on the use of writing assignments in history, physics, mathematics, painting, computer-aided drafting, computer, vocational, and biology courses.

Dana Nicole Williams is a staff writer at the ERIC Clearinghouse for Junior Colleges.

INDEX

ORDERING INFORMATION

NEW DIRECTIONS FOR COMMUNITY COLLEGES is a series of paperback books that provides expert assistance to help community colleges meet the challenges of their distinctive and expanding educational mission. Books in the series are published quarterly in Fall, Winter, Spring, and Summer and are available for purchase by subscription as well as by single copy.

SUBSCRIPTIONS for 1991 cost $48.00 for individuals (a savings of 20 percent over single-copy prices) and $70.00 for institutions, agencies, and libraries. Please do not send institutional checks for personal subscriptions. Standing orders are accepted.

SINGLE COPIES cost $15.95 when payment accompanies order. (California, New Jersey, New York, and Washington, D.C., residents please include appropriate sales tax.) Billed orders will be charged postage and handling.

DISCOUNTS FOR QUANTITY ORDERS are available. Please write to the address below for information.

ALL ORDERS must include either the name of an individual or an official purchase order number. Please submit your order as follows:
    Subscriptions: specify series and year subscription is to begin
    Single copies: include individual title code (such as CC1)

MAIL ALL ORDERS TO:
    Jossey-Bass Inc., Publishers
    350 Sansome Street
    San Francisco, California 94104

OTHER TITLES AVAILABLE IN THE
NEW DIRECTIONS FOR COMMUNITY COLLEGES SERIES
Arthur M. Cohen, Editor-in-Chief
Florence B. Brawer, Associate Editor

MODELS FOR CONDUCTING INSTITUTIONAL RESEARCH
Peter R. MacDougall, Jack Friedlander (eds.)
New Directions for Community Colleges, no. 72, Winter 1990
Volume XVIII, number 4
San Francisco: Jossey-Bass.

ERRATUM

The Table of Contents was printed incorrectly in the above volume. All subscribers will receive a replacement volume number 72 with a corrected Table of Contents. We apologize for any inconvenience this error may have caused.